JAINISM

JAINISM

From Bhagavān Mahāvīra to Mahatma Gandhi

PANKAJ JAIN

INDIAN INSTITUTE OF ADVANCED STUDY, SHIMLA

MANOHAR
2026

First published 2026
First eBook edition 2026

ISBN 978-93-6080-603-3 (hardbound)
ISBN 978-93-6080-730-6 (eBook)

Published by the Deputy Secretary
Indian Institute of Advanced Study
Rashtrapati Nivas, Shimla
and
Ajay Kumar Jain *for*
Manohar Publishers & Distributors
4753/23 Ansari Road, Daryaganj
New Delhi 110002

Typeset by Ravi Shanker, Delhi 110095

Cover design by Manoj Kumar

Printed and bound in India

Contents

Prologue 9

Introduction: Modern Jainism – Dharma of Sustainability and Sustainability of Dharma 13

The Influence of Jain Virtue Ethics on India's Sustainability and Environmental Issues 15

Jain Role Models and their Inspiration for Virtue Ethics 19

Gandhi and other Examples of Jain Virtue Ethics for Sustainability 21

Social Action and Sustainability in Modern Jainism 22

Mahāvīra in Academic Literature 26

1. *Chyavana* and *Janma*: Conception, Birth and Early Years 29

Disputes and Controversies 31

Birthplace 35

Parents 36

Adolescence 37

Marriage 38

2. *Dīkṣā*: Renunciation 41
The First Day as an Ascetic 42
The First Year of Penance 44
The Second Year of Penance 47
The Third Year of Penance 51
The Fourth Year of Penance 51
The Fifth Year of Penance 53
The Sixth Year of Penance 54
The Seventh Year of Penance 55
The Eighth Year of Penance 55
The Ninth Year of Penance 56
The Tenth Year of Penance 56
The Eleventh Year of Penance 57
The Twelfth Year of Penance 58

3. *Keval Jñāna*: Omniscience 62
The First Year as the Tīrthaṅkara 63
The Second Year as the Tīrthaṅkara 64
The Third Year as the Tīrthaṅkara 64
The Fourth Year as the Tīrthaṅkara 66
The Fifth Year as the Tīrthaṅkara 66
The Sixth Year as the Tīrthaṅkara 67
The Seventh Year as the Tīrthaṅkara 67
The Eighth Year as the Tīrthaṅkara 68
The Ninth Year as the Tīrthaṅkara 68
The Tenth Year as the Tīrthaṅkara 69
The Eleventh Year as the Tīrthaṅkara 70
The Twelfth Year as the Tīrthaṅkara 71
The Thirteenth Year as the Tīrthaṅkara 71
The Fourteenth Year as the Tīrthaṅkara 72

The Fifteenth Year as the Tīrthaṅkara 72
The Sixteenth Year as the Tīrthaṅkara 75
The Seventeenth Year as the Tīrthaṅkara 78
The Eighteenth Year as the Tīrthaṅkara 78
The Nineteenth Year as the Tīrthaṅkara 81
The Twentieth Year as the Tīrthaṅkara 81
The Twenty-first Year as the Tīrthaṅkara 82
The Twenty-second Year as the Tīrthaṅkara 83
The Twenty-third Year as the Tīrthaṅkara 84
The Twenty-fourth Year as the Tīrthaṅkara 84
The Twenty-fifth Year as the Tīrthaṅkara 85
The Twenty-sixth Year as the Tīrthaṅkara 86
The Twenty-seventh Year as the Tīrthaṅkara 86
The Twenty-eighth Year as the Tīrthaṅkara 87
The Twenty-ninth Year as the Tīrthaṅkara 87
The Thirtieth Year as the Tīrthaṅkara 87

4. *Parinirvāṇa*: Liberation 91
Mahāvīra's Chief Male Disciples 92
Mahāvīra's First Female Disciple 95
Historical Analysis of Mahāvīra's Nirvāṇa 96
Historical Analysis of the Years of the Buddha's and Mahāvīra's Nirvāṇa 97

5. Jainism, Dharma, and Environmental Ethics 101
Introduction 101
Bishnoi Community and Jainism 109
Examples of Non-violent Environmentalism 111

Bibliography 121

Index 129

Prologue

Mahāvīra was the twenty-fourth Tīrthaṅkara, sometimes translated as fordmaker, in the Jain tradition and was a contemporary of Lord Buddha. Like the Buddha, Mahāvīra also organised the community in *Saṃgha* and sent his disciples to spread the dharma, as mentioned in BKB (1.50) (Jain 1945: 8). His householder male disciples numbered 1,59,000,[1] female householders 318,000, monks 14,000, and nuns 36,000. Seven hundred people in his congregation became omniscient.[2] He spent thirty years as a householder and forty-two years as an ascetic, out of his total lifespan of seventy-two years. His final fast was for two days, after which he left his body to attain liberation.[3]

While Buddhism is a worldwide phenomenon with several books available on the Buddha's biography,[4] searching for a similar book on Mahāvīra yields little results, especially in English. Like the charismatic authority of other religious traditions, Mahāvīra continues to influence Jainism, but the absence of literature about his life is conspicuous by its absence.[5] As Kragh (2011) notes, biographical narratives are not a hallmark of Jain texts. Like most ancient Indian legendary figures, biographies of Jain Tīrthaṅkaras are compiled from the Jain canon of several texts accepted by the Shvetambara sect. Digambaras, on the other hand, have an alternative set of ancient texts which became the source for their version of Jain Tīrthaṅkaras' biographies. For this monograph, I have consulted various secondary sources in English, Hindi and Gujarati, and the primary sources in Prakrit and Sanskrit, as listed in the Bibliography. Jain tradition marks five milestones of the Tīrthaṅkaras by calling them *Panch Kalyāṇaka,* which are conception (*Chyavana*), birth (*Janma*), renunciation (*Dīkṣā*), omniscience (*Kevala Jñāna*), and liberation (*Mokṣa*). Accordingly, this monograph is divided into different chapters as we dig into various events in Mahāvīra's life.

In line with my earlier book on the biographies of Jain saints (Jain 2023), this book is inspired and supported by my family, friends, colleagues, and students. I am grateful for the research grants provided by FLAME University, its student Nandhini Somasundaram for her research and editorial assistance, and the fellow at the India Centre, Dr. Sanchari Basu Chaudhuri, for her editorial suggestions. I thank the fellowship support provided by the Indian Institute of Advanced Studies in Shimla for this project and for publishing an article from my manuscript in their review journal, *Summer Hill*. I am grateful for permission from Prof. Dharmachand Jain to translate Acharya Hastimal's biographical chapter of Mahāvīra, which is extensively used for the biographical chapters, including the citations, for compiling Mahāvīra's biography in this monograph. The permission to republish my chapter from Oxford University Press[6] is gratefully acknowledged.

NOTES

1. According to the Digambara texts, male householder disciples were 1,00,000 and female 3,00,000.
2. He had the lowest number of disciples, including householders, monks and nuns, compared to his twenty-three predecessors. Number of omniscient is also the lowest (Hastīmal 1971: 818).

3. All his time spans are lower compared to his twenty-three predecessors.
4. Karen Armstrong's biography of the Buddha (2002) is the inspirations for this book.
5. His life story is briefly referenced in academic books on Jainism (e.g., Dundas 2002; Jaini 1979; Long 2008).
6. Portions of the manuscript appeared as 'Jain Dharma as Virtue Ethics for Sustainability', in *The Virtues of Sustainability*, edited by Jason Kawall, Oxford University Press, 2021. Other portions also appeared as Pankaj Jain, 'Jainism, Dharma, and Environmental Ethics', in *Union Seminary Quarterly Review*, 61.1, 2011, pp. 121-35.

Introduction

Modern Jainism: Dharma of Sustainability and Sustainability of Dharma

In her presidential address at the American Political Science Association's annual meeting, Susanne Rudolph mentioned (2005):

> Early in our research in India, Lloyd Rudolph and I coined the phrase 'imperialism of categories'. It was meant to designate the academic practice of imposing concepts on the other – the export of concepts as part of a hegemonic relationship. Categories crafted in a dominant socio-cultural environment are exported to a subordinate one. The imperialism of categories entails an unself-conscious parochialism of categories: scholars from a dominant culture, sometimes called the centre, travel to a distant and lesser place, sometimes called the periphery, where they apply 'universal' concepts. The trouble is that the concepts have been fashioned out of the centre. The East is fatalist, says Max Weber; the West is agentic. The non-West conveys status by birth, says Talcott Parsons, the West, by achievement. The non-West is childlike, says John Stuart Mill; the West is mature. Dominant peoples use ideal types and stereotypes to control the dominated by ranking and creating cultural and social registers.

To avoid such 'imperialism of categories' and following Gerald Larson (2004) and McKim Marriott (1990), in this chapter,

I begin by noting that terms such as philosophy, religion, ethics, sustainability, and environmentalism are obviously all, English terms and etymologically based on Greco-Roman intellectual heritage and Judeo-Christian religious heritage. All such ideas remain intertwined in much of the non-Western world, such as Asia and Africa. For instance, in all the texts in Indian history and contexts from contemporary communities in India, it can be a useless exercise to explore where philosophy ends and where religion begins or vice versa. In these descriptions and prescriptions for thinking and living in the world, philosophy and religion overlap, and sustainability and environmentalism remain an undercurrent, adding a third layer to this combination of philosophy and religion.

Among the ancient religions of the world, Jainism and Buddhism are usually categorised as non-theistic religions. In this chapter, I will explore how *karma* theory and virtues such as non-violence guide Jains in their actions. Rather than investigating Dharma's 'virtue ethics' for sustainability, we can begin by looking at the Jain way of life. This tradition brings to our attention unique examples, such as some monks renouncing their clothes. Most Jain lay people have been vegetarian for more than twenty-six hundred years, millennia before it became a trend elsewhere in the world. The last great teacher in the Jaiṇ tradition was Mahāvīra, a contemporary of the Buddha (living around sixth century BCE). The combined influence of Buddhism and Jainism has profoundly shaped Indian society, most evidently in the practice of vegetarianism that millions of Indians continue to practice today in India and now across the world among the diaspora. While Buddhism also encourages non-violence and vegetarianism, Jainism puts the ultimate emphasis on this ideal. It defines religion or philosophy as non-violence with its great mantra, *Ahimsa Paramo Dharma* 'Non-violence is the supreme virtue, ethic and religion'.

In America, non-violence is most closely associated with Dr. Martin Luther King, who based his Civil Rights Movement on this principle. Dr. King and a few other African-American leaders visited Gandhi's home in India and brought the Gandhian ideal of non-violence to America (Lakshmi 2009). Gandhi, in turn, was influenced by Jainism. So, some scholars have referred to Jainism with the three M's who emphasised the principle of non-violence: Mahāvīra (the last celebrated teacher contemporary of the Buddha), Mahatma (Gandhi), and Martin (Helton 2007; King 1999; Nojeim 2004). Thus, at least in two ways, Jainism's non-violence remains relevant in the contemporary United States: the enduring influence of Dr. King's method of non-violent resistance and increasing awareness for vegetarianism. In the last decade, there have been several reports from the United Nations[1] and other agencies connecting meat consumption with climate change, especially factory farming, which is now widely seen as one of the extreme examples of cruelty against animals and, in turn, towards our planet.

THE INFLUENCE OF JAIN VIRTUE ETHICS ON INDIA'S SUSTAINABILITY AND ENVIRONMENTAL ISSUES

Prima facie, one can be appalled by the large-scale destruction and pollution of India's natural resources. The assault on land is visible everywhere. The forest areas are under tremendous pressure, especially as villagers continue to look for their daily firewood and fodder in their natural environment. The encroachment of such open areas is also a severe threat. Industrial pollution in India is akin to what happened to American cities such as Pittsburgh in the 1940s (Davidson 1979). For instance, one can also notice that unplanned urbanisation leads to waste disposal issues. There are several large-scale projects with significant impacts, such as large dams, which do not necessarily rehabilitate and relocate the displaced Indigenous people from such sites. The pollution in Indian rivers can remind one of the American rivers, such as Ohio's Cuyahoga in the 1960s (Rotman 2010).

However, to present an alternative picture of India's environment, we can look at the Greendex survey conducted by National Geographic between 2008 and 2014 (Greendex 2009). In these surveys, India consistently appears as the 'greenest' country, greener than the United States and other Western countries, and greener than China and Brazil, and other developing countries. The criterion that kept India greener than other countries is the national carbon footprint of Indians, which remains lower than their counterparts elsewhere, based on broad parameters such as consumption in terms of housing needs, transportation needs, food and other consumer goods. In each of these four categories, many Indians continue to keep their carbon footprint lower than people elsewhere. This frugal lifestyle of Indians used to be critiqued by economists (sometimes disparagingly) by labelling it as the 'Hindu rate of economic growth'. These economists lamented that Indians consumed fewer natural resources than their counterparts elsewhere because of lower per capita income levels and the influence of philosophical and cultural traditions such as Hinduism. Be that as it may, one can undoubtedly note that the dietary habits of many Indians were influenced more than two thousand years ago when the great leaders of Buddhism and Jainism, the Buddha and Mahāvīra, respectively, emphasised non-violence towards animals as one of the supreme virtues. Over time, most Indians stopped sacrificing animals in their rituals, and today, they depend on rice, wheat, lentils, fruits and vegetables for their staple diet (although some of them might choose a non-vegetarian meal occasionally). So, while economists critiqued the 'Hindu rate of growth', environmentalists should celebrate the 'Hindu-Jain way of life' that keeps India's carbon footprint lower than that of other countries. In the rest of this chapter, I will explore the rationale for Jain virtue ethics from the sustainability perspective.

The Jain cosmology divides all the beings in the universe into two categories, living (*jiva*) and non-living (*ajiva*), and space into two categories, the living abode (*loka*) and non-living abode (*aloka*). In this cosmology, in addition to humans, animals, birds, insects, reptiles, and even earth, fire, air and water are Jiva, i.e. with distinct and unique souls. The prominent non-living beings, in addition to the medium of motion, medium of rest, time and space, are the *karma* particles that pollute the souls of most of us because of the violence that we commit, intentionally or unintentionally, as we live in the world. Since the complete cessation of violence is impossible for any living being, out of one, two, three, four and five-sensed beings, Jainism encouraged humans to consume only one-sensed beings (Chapple 2002, 128). These are earth, air, fire, water and plants with only one sense of touch. Five-sensed beings include mammals (including humans) and birds.[2] Jainism's rationale for non-violence equates humans with other mammals and birds, so for a human to kill any animal or bird would accrue the same *karma* as killing a fellow human being.

Further, for human living, even one-sensed beings such as earth, water, air, fire and plants should be consumed with the utmost care. Among plants, vegetables such as carrots, radishes, onions and garlic are discouraged because destroying a stem or root kills the entire plant. Similarly, only filtered water is to be consumed to avoid any violence to microbes in the water. Some Jain monks and nuns cover their mouths as they speak and breathe to prevent any harm to microbes in the air. Many devout Jains avoid eating after sunset to minimise the energy consumption from burning fossil fuels. Similarly, Jain monks and nuns avoid riding vehicles as well. Based on similar concerns for one-sensed beings, many Jains actively try to preserve wildlands, keep waterways and air unpolluted, and address climate change.

In addition to *Ahimsā* (non-violence), *Aparigraha* (non-accumulation of materials) is the most important ideal that has inspired Jain virtue ethics in its long history. Just as non-violence finds its most clear application in vegetarianism, *Aparigraha* finds its application in the Jain insistence on minimising worldly possessions, as explained in the second book of one of the earliest Jain texts *Ācārāṅga Sūtra* (Dundas 2003:159). In an article for the *Washington Post* (14 December 2006), Diana Eck quoted Gandhi's words, 'The earth has enough for one's need but not for one's greed.' Gandhi practised what he preached by limiting his possessions and even his necessities.

Several Jains have also donated large sums of their hard-earned wealth to philanthropic causes such as education, healthcare, disaster relief, orphanages, and animal shelters, to name a few. Lay Jains have continued to support and revere their monks and nuns as their ultimate role models for *Aparigraha*. Indeed, some monks go to the extreme of renouncing every piece of cloth and utensils for eating their food. They walk entirely naked and eat a small meal with their bare hands because even collecting food or wearing clothes may turn into attachments and some violence towards natural resources. Such monks continue to inspire thousands of Jains to carry the ideal of *Aparigraha* in high esteem and a goal to achieve as they hope to progress in their spiritual journey. Non-violence, non-accumulation, and non-possession also serve as high virtues for Jains to sustain our planetary resources.

The third crucial Jain virtue, *Anekāntavāda*, means the doctrine of pluralism or 'many pointedness' (Dundas 2003: 229). This virtue continues to inspire Jains to practice intellectual non-violence by trying to keep an open mind toward different philosophical and religious traditions. The parable of an elephant and six blind men explains this virtue well. As these men touch different parts of the elephant, they equate the elephant with a snake (the man touching its tail), a wall (the man touching its belly), and a spear (the man touching its tusk). However, the holistic definition of an elephant is possible only by combining all these partial definitions. *Anekāntavāda* similarly has inspired Jains to learn and preserve their rival ideologies of Hinduism and Buddhism for centuries. Because of this open mind, Jains did not hesitate to interact with Islamic emperors and even partially succeeded in occasionally making them adopt non-violence as the state policy, as noted below. The virtue of *Anekāntavāda* also applies to sustainability by inspiring Jains to consider natural resources from non-anthropocentric perspectives. For instance, in India, many have observed that even the national highways are open for animals, unlike the American national highways, where humans are not allowed to 'loiter'. Why should humans monopolise the roads or any other planetary resource? *Anekāntavāda* encourages us to accept even the animals' perspectives towards the highways, water, or other natural resources.

Jainism's *Anekāntavāda* can help achieve cooperation and sustainability. For example, as it requires thinking about others' perspectives, it could be conducive to encouraging social sustainability and alliances for environmental sustainability. Non-violence and pluralism might also be very important for sustainability in terms of allowing diverse communities to tolerate and respect each other and to work together for sustainability.

JAIN ROLE MODELS AND THEIR INSPIRATION FOR VIRTUE ETHICS

As aforementioned, Mahāvīra (~600 BCE), the great hero, was the 24th and the last great teacher of Jainism and was a contemporary of the Buddha. Many of his statements and actions concerning compassion for trees and animals continue to inspire many Jains to be protectors of animals and nature in general, even today. For instance, one of the prominent Jain sacred texts, *Ācārāṅga Sūtra,* records his statements such as 'trees are inherently valuable' (2.4.2.11-12) and 'vegetation has a life just as humans' (1.1.5.9-11). In his last moments, Mahāvīra sent one of his foremost disciples, Indrabhuti, to stop cattle slaughter.

In Jain cosmology, there are twenty-four such great teachers in every era. Before Mahāvīra, the 22nd teacher, Neminatha, and the 23rd teacher, Parshvanatha, renounced their royal families and wealth after encountering violence against animals and reptiles, respectively. Other Jain sacred texts such as *Tattvārtha Sūtra* and *Bhavāni Sūtra* have statements such as, 'The souls render service to one another.' Another verse from *Dashavaikālika Sūtra* (1.2-5) highlights the behaviour of bees of collecting only minimal nectar from each flower instead of damaging or destroying the flower. Humans should also preserve their natural resources and consume them minimally for their existence. Another text, *Adipurāna,* states, 'Forests are like saints, and Trees should be planted for positive karma.'

Such examples and role models have continued to inspire Jain householders to get involved in less violent professions such as trading, banking, administrative activities, traditional medicine, arts and crafts, publishing, and education. According to an ancient Jain text, *Bhogopabhog Vrata*, one would rarely, if ever, find a Jain householder involved in more violent professions such as trading of charcoal, alcohol, enslaved people, weapons, poisons, sugar canes, firearms, or timber. Jains have stayed away from exploiting animals or constructing lakes, as such activities also involve causing great violence to the environment.

GANDHI AND OTHER EXAMPLES OF JAIN VIRTUE ETHICS FOR SUSTAINABILITY

Mahatma Gandhi remains the most prominent role model who practised and preached the virtue ethics of sustainability based on Jainism (and other philosophical traditions). Vinay Lal (2000) describes Gandhi as 'too deep' even for deep ecology. According to Lal, by leading a virtuous life, Gandhi is a role model of environmentalism that goes far beyond what 'deep ecology' advocates. Although Gandhi left for South Africa in 1891, he continued to correspond with a Jain guru, Shrimad Rajchandra, for several years. He adopted several ideas in his movement against the British colonial and racist policies against Indians in South Africa and later in India. Some of these virtues were the truth (*Satya*), non-violence (*Ahimsa*), non-accumulation (*Aparigraha*), celibacy (*Brahmacharya*), self-reliance (*Purushartha*), and fasting (*Upavasa*). Gandhi's life emerged as an ecological treatise, a living ecosystem manifested by his lifelong practices such as his small meals of nuts and fruits, daily ablutions and bodily practices, periodic observances of silence, morning walks, spinning wheel, and waste avoidance. Today, many moralists, non-violent activists, feminists, journalists, social reformers, trade union leaders, peasants, prohibitionists, nature-cure lovers, renouncers, and environmentalists continue to be inspired by Gandhi's life.

Long before Gandhi, Emperor Aśoka erected dozens of edicts across India to proclaim non-violence in his empire by maintaining sacred groves and prohibiting hunting and violence (Dhammika 1993). Although Aśoka adopted Buddhism, his grandfather Chandragupta Maurya (*Britannica* 2009) and grandson Samprati (Dundas 2003, 115) had adopted Jainism, according to Jainism's historical sources. Similarly, an emperor in Gujarat, Siddharaja, and his successor, Kumarapala, promoted Jainism and non-violence in the medieval period in Indian history. Islamic emperors such as Muhammad Tughluq, Akbar, and Jahangir also periodically prohibited hunting and meat consumption for some special days under the influence of Jain monks who visited their courts.

SOCIAL ACTION AND SUSTAINABILITY IN MODERN JAINISM

As Flugel (2005) notes, Jains have been active in social activism in their long history. Recent prominent Jain leaders and spokespersons demonstrate Jainism's adherence to non-violence, such as the late Jain monks Sushil Muni and Acharya Tulsi, who opposed geopolitical conflicts, terrorism, and other socio-political violence. As Cort (2002) notes, hundreds of thousands of Jains perform a ritual called *Pratikraman* every day in which they ask for forgiveness from 8.4 million species, including the one-sensed, two-sensed, three-sensed, four-sensed and five-sensed beings for any intentional or unintentional violence committed in action, speech, or thought.[3] If understood sincerely, this ritual can help remind and transform some of those Jains involved in industries that are polluting and damaging to local natural resources. Many Jains support and fund hundreds of shelters and hospitals for animals and birds across India and North America (Lodrick 1981). The Bird Hospital in New Delhi remains among the most celebrated efforts (Andersen 2019). Since its establishment in 1956, the local Jains have continued supporting and managing this avian veterinary hospital that treats thousands of sick and injured birds yearly.

Khichan, a small village in the desert of the Indian state Rajasthan, has similarly caught the attention of several birdwatchers as the local Jains there welcome and feed thousands of Demoiselle Cranes that visit this village from across Asia. Another example is from Goa in India, where the largest wildlife sanctuary was named after Mahāvīra, the last great teacher of Jainism, and the local Jains there contributed a large sum of money to this cause (Jain 2011). Jains continue to promote vegetarianism and push for a ban on meat consumption across the world. According to several recent news reports, many Jain temples such as those in Byculla, Dahanu, Nashik, Shahpur (Maharashtra), Dilwara (Rajasthan), Kolaththur (Tamil Nadu), Bareilly (Uttar Pradesh), Franklin (New Jersey), and Milpitas (California) have adopted solar energy to reduce their carbon footprint. Other Jain temples, such as those in Detroit, Michigan, and Dallas, Texas, have also taken other green measures to reflect the virtue of non-violence towards nature. Other Indian Jain temples, such as Shatrunjaya Temple in Palitana and Veerayatan, Bihar, have initiated reforestation in their surroundings. The Jain Center of Southern California holds ongoing events in support of animal rights. The Detroit Jain Temple works with the Sasha Farm, the Midwest's most significant animal sanctuary, housing over two hundred rescued and aged animals near Ann Arbor, Michigan. Other American Jains are active in the Vegetarian Society of the District of Columbia and with another cattle sanctuary managed by the Voith Family of Angelica, New York (Vallely 2002).

One of the most prominent examples of animal shelters is Shree Sumati Jeev Raksha Kendra in Rajasthan.[4] A leading Jain group and other Jain donors manage this cattle sanctuary.[5] The campus is over 7 million square feet and includes a Jain temple. This centre started in 1998, with around 100 cattle and now houses more than 6,000 animals that are cared for by 175 employees. Unlike North American cattle farms that are slaughtered for human consumption, the cattle at this centre are managed according to Jainism's principle of feeding them only vegetarian food. These cattle are maintained in a sacred environment where Jain chants continuously play on loudspeakers. The centre runs on biogas produced here using cow dung from the cattle . The water needs of the centre are fulfilled by rainwater harvesting at the centre itself. Food for the animals is locally grown, and the milk from the cows is fed to their calves. The centre also supports and feeds local birds and stray dogs. The centre has also planted more than 100,000 trees in its vicinity, including some of the sacred trees of the Jain tradition.[6]

Scholars and practitioners need to study these phenomena in Jainism that have now become global in scope. For example, consider the contemporary Jain leaders who are taking the values of Jainism to the new frontier of veganism. Although most Jain ascetics are vegetarians, we now have several activists and mendicants who embrace non-violence at an even deeper level through veganism. Pradeep Shah, Founder of Nature's Law and Diet System[7] in Mumbai, is one of the many prominent Jain activists organising talks by Jain ascetics on veganism. Jain ascetics such as Labdhi Sagar, Vaibhav Shree,[8] Viharsh Sagar, Aryika Chaitanyamati,[9] and Dev Nandi are spearheading the Vegan movement inspired by the Jain principle of non-violence. Some active websites, such as VeganJains.com and JainVegans.org, promote veganism among Jains and others. Several UK-based Jain groups are turning vegan. USA-born Jains frequently organise vegan panels at various Jain conventions and their local temples. For a glimpse of such efforts, my translation of the Gujarati discourse by Labdhi Sagar in Mumbai is mentioned below. Some claims made by him may be extreme, as I am sharing my verbatim translation from an excerpt of his recorded lecture on 13 August 2017:

> Today, we treat cattle like raw materials and exploit and torture them to the extreme for maximum output. In Jainism, we are for-

bidden to take anything from other beings without their consent. Our gurus advise us against such actions, and we accumulate much negative *karma* if we continue. Such actions will lead to premature death in the next lives, as explained by the Jain principle of *karma*, action, and consequence. Even the government does not share the exact statistics about the number of animals used in the dairy and meat industry. However, according to the Food Safety and Standards Authority of India (FSSAI), 75% of Indian milk is contaminated with chemicals such as urea, caustic soda, paints, detergent powder, sodium chloride, and shampoo. We should consume milk in minimal quantity, and the milk must be obtained from the cattle treated like family.

The 2002 edited book *Jainism and Ecology: Nonviolence in the Web of Life* was the first significant attempt in the Western hemisphere to study Jainism from an environmental perspective. However, most of the epistemological and hermeneutic methodologies applied by scholars, such as Cort, on non-Western traditions such as Jainism are rooted in the Western categories. The Western categories must be broadened by incorporating Indic terms in English, such as *Prakriti*, *Jiva*, and *Ahimsa*. Western scholarship must also look at the living laboratories of the ecological, sustainable sensibilities in lives such as Gandhi's, which defy all neat categories of being an environmentalist, a philosopher, or an activist. The non-violence-based inspiration from Mahāvīra (Swami) to Mahatma (Gandhi) has continued to Martin (Luther King) and several other contemporary leaders such as Sunderlal Bahuguna and Nelson Mandela, and it is high time that scholars of religion and ecology embrace this *Ahimsak* Ecology, nonviolent environmental ethics, and not just Deep Ecology. Although no religion can claim to have anticipated our current environmental situation, contemporary Jain vegans are inspired by Jainism's non-violence. They can be seen as a unique response to the ongoing sustainability crisis.

MAHĀVĪRA IN ACADEMIC LITERATURE

At the time of writing this monograph, Paul Dundas's (2020) 16000-word article is the most comprehensive material on the history of the 23rd and 24th Tīrthaṅkaras, Pārśva and Mahāvīra. Interestingly, in this article, he avoided the term he coined 'fordmaker' for Tīrthaṅkara for his earlier major book, *The Jains* (2002). In this article, he used the term *Jina* instead of fordmaker. However, as widely known, not all Jinas are Tīrthaṅkara, although the reverse is true. Therefore, Jina cannot be synonymously used for Tīrthaṅkara.[10] Jina refers to anyone attaining omniscience, but Tīrthaṅkara denotes those Jinas who establish the four-fold community of laymen, laywomen, monks and nuns, all of whom follow the teachings and role models of the Tīrthaṅkara.

To my surprise, Dundas ignored many recent biographical texts of Jain Tīrthaṅkaras in Hindi and other Indian languages, even though many of them are relevant with citations from Jain canonical texts. There has been a long-standing issue with Western Indology that jumps directly from Sanskrit or Prakrit texts to English, ignoring that ancient traditions continue to be practised vibrantly across India and the Indian diaspora spread worldwide in the tweny-first century. In the present monograph, I attempt to locate Mahāvīra not just from Prakrit or Sanskrit sources but also study how he continues to be portrayed by contemporary authors in Hindi and other Indian languages. Dundase begins his article by noting, 'the Jains have never developed any sort of reflexive science of history', which can be generalised to all religious traditions with several millennia of history instead of singling out Jains. He notes that 'localised versions of the Jain past' . . . 'have been regularly produced over the last millennium'. However, such texts were written before 'the last millennium' also. As widely known, the Śvētāmbara scriptures, such as KS, started this tradition over two thousand years ago with different Tīrthaṅkaras' biographical details, which Dundas reviews in several ways throughout the article. This article does not provide detailed biographical information about Mahāvīra and pedantically glances at various historical disputes related to different notions of his life. The more problematic issue is that the article completely discards the twenty-two Tīrthaṅkaras that are mentioned as predecessors to the 23rd and 24th Tīrthaṅkaras, Pārśva and Mahāvīra and discards their existence as fictional. I wonder if figures over three thousand years old in other traditions and cultures are treated with similar antipathy, or at least a window is kept open for further exploration and research into that hoary past? Also, Western academics have yet to study the seals and images found in the Indus Valley sites from the Jain perspective, especially those resembling naked Jinas (Jain n.d.).

NOTES

1. http://www.fao.org/news/story/en/item/197623/icode/, accessed on 1 January 2025.
2. According to Jainism, two-sensed beings are worms, leeches, oysters, and snails with lifespan of twelve years, three-sensed beings are insects and spiders with lifespan of forty-nine days, and four-sensed beings are butterflies, flies, and bees with lifespan of six months.
3. Although the total number of species according to the latest scientific research is approximately 8.7 million (±1.3 million) according to Mora et al. (2011), the number of species in all the ancient Indian texts is mentioned to be 8.4 million. If biologists tell us that there are over 10 million species, Jains would respect and seek forgiveness from all of them.
4. http://www.pavapuri.com/#animals, accessed on 20 March 2019.
5. https://www.jaina.org/page/JivDaya in 2017, North American Jains donated around $50,000 to such animal shelters across India and in North America, accessed on 20 March 2019.

6. In my 2011 article, I explore several such cattle sanctuaries across India.
7. https://www.youtube.com/channel/UCuVwIzDOODc_vU8EkmfWwYw (accessed on 17 May 2019).
8. https://www.youtube.com/watch?v=DLyitfLJ6vk (accessed on 17 May 2019).
9. https://m.facebook.com/story.php?story_fbid=10156108359347120&id=545827119 (accessed on 17 June 2019).
10. https://jainworld.com/library/jain-books/books-on-line/jainworld-books-in-indian-languages/24-tirthankaras/who-is-a-tirthankar/ (accessed on 15 May 2023).

CHAPTER 1

Chyavana and *Janma*
Conception, Birth and Early Years

The Jain tradition has definite spatial boundaries with a universe, *Loka,* and a non-universe, *Aloka.* However, it has no temporal boundaries – no beginning or end and runs according to the cosmic time cycle *ad infinitum*. It has twenty-four Tīrthaṅkaras in each cycle, and Mahāvīra was born in 599 BCE (Dundas 2002: 24), approximately two hundred and fifty years after his predecessor Pārśva, the 23rd Tīrthaṅkara.[1] Being the 24th Tīrthaṅkara, Mahāvīra is not the founder of Jainism, but it was only after him that Jains eventually developed a distinct identity of a separate religious community.[2] Unlike him, the 1st Jain Tīrthaṅkara, Ṛṣabha, is mentioned as an incarnation of Viṣṇu, a principal Hindu deity (Jaini 1977). Padmāvatī, a guardian deity for the 23rd Tīrthaṅkara Pārśva, is worshipped by some Hindus also, and the 22nd Tīrthaṅkara Nemi, according to the Jain texts, is a cousin of Kriṣṇa, the crucial figure in the *Mahābhārata*. This ecumenical spirit disappeared with the advent of Mahāvīra, who added innovative ideas and practices to the tradition of the earlier 23 Tīrthaṅkaras. Like him, Buddha became the founder of another new religious tradition from the same region of north India. Dundas (2020: 119) cites Hermann Jacobi and notes Pārśva as the founder of Jainism without much clarification or explanation.

The contemporary socio-religious accounts indicate that animal sacrifice was rampant in most of the Vedic rituals of that era, as advocated by some of the verses in the *Manusmriti* (*MS* 5: 22: 39-44). Brahmins were revered and regarded as pure as the divine fire, and they dominated the religious affairs (MS 9: 317-19). Licchavikas led one of the prominent republic empires, Vajjika League (Aquique 1978: 126), whose capital was Vaiśālī, located in the present Indian state of Bihar. According to some Buddhist texts, this republic was spread across 2,300 square miles, and the seventh-century Chinese Buddhist traveller Xuan Zang mentioned its area to be 5,000 square miles (Jain 1998). He also praised the socio-economic prosperity of this region. According to the historian Vincent Arthur Smith, Licchavikas migrated from Tibet, while Indologist Brian Houghton Hodgson considered them Scythians from Central Asia. However, texts in Jainism and Buddhism portray them as native Kṣatriyas of northern India (Jain 1998).

Mahāvīra's mother, Triśalā, was the sister of Chetak, the consul (or Prime Minister) of the Licchavis. She is also referred to elsewhere as one of Chetak's daughters.

Like the incomplete biographical details of the early lives of Siddhārtha Gautama, Jesus and Muhammad (Armstrong 2002), Mahāvīra's life is also shrouded by a lack of historical facts. Charismatic authorities (Weber 1963) start their career not with their biological birth but with their messianic birth. Their biographies (and hagiographies) start with their significant heroic departure, gain momentum with their journey, and end with their liberation (Campbell 2020). As suggested by Turner (1968) and like the Bodhisattva notion in Mahayana Buddhism, Jain Tīrthaṅkara achieves omniscience and, out of compassion for others, facilitates a community of ascetics and lay-people of all classes, castes and genders. Like the Hindu notion of *Avatāra* (incarnation), some have speculated that Jain Tīrthaṅkaras also choose to take birth for the larger good of society. Followers of his predecessor Pārśva accepted Mahāvīra,[3] but even today, they prefer the former as the central image in their Śvētāmbara temples. In contrast, Digambara temples do not show any preference for Pārśva. Dundas (2020: 116, 118) makes a generic statement about more devotion towards Pārśva without noticing this sectarian difference. Mahāvīra as the central image is more prevalent in Digambara temples. The sectarian differences continue in many ways, as mentioned later in this chapter.

DISPUTES AND CONTROVERSIES

Adolescent Mahāvīra was known as Vardhamāna, i.e. the growing one. Although some have speculated that the name signified the materialistic growth in his family (ibid.: 126),[4] the name may also underscore that the only event happening in his life was his silent natural growth. Like the myths about the birth of Buddha and other charismatic authorities, Mahāvīra's mother also had several auspicious dreams prophesising the birth of the Tīrthaṅkara.[5] Unfortunately, such dreams are not yet psychoanalysed for their proper interpretation, especially compared to dreams of mothers who gave birth to other kinds of personalities such as Hitler or Stalin. Interestingly, Mahāvīra's father summoned experts to interpret these dreams, who predicted that the child would bring a great name to the family lineage.

In addition to the dreams, there is an additional myth about the womb transfer in the Śvētāmbara texts (but not in the Digambara texts). According to Georges Dumezil's Trifunctional Hypothesis (1988), many Indo-European societies had three dominant classes – priests, warriors and commoners. Brahmins dominated the religious rituals in India, and Kṣatriyas sponsored the rituals with generous donations. Perhaps emphasising the categorical rejection of the Brahminical authority, Mahāvīra's parents were Kṣatriyas, not Brahmins, as the womb was transferred from the Brahmin mother to the Kṣatriya mother. Coward (1985) states that the Hindu *varnas* influenced Jungian psychological typology. A Brahminical personality model is based on a personality type dependent on others.

In contrast, a Kṣatriya model is based on the personality types that demonstrate martial powers leaning towards battle and conquest. The spiritual path chosen by Mahāvīra and his twenty-three earlier Tīrthaṅkaras demonstrated a sense of victory, albeit not over others but over themselves and were called Jinas, the victors. Therefore, all of them were mentioned to be born in the Kṣatriya lineage instead of Brahminical. In one of the Jain texts, a Brahmin couple is referred to as the biological parents of Mahāvīra. However, as all Jain texts describe, a child destined to follow a Kṣatriya model of conquering himself must grow in a Kṣatriya milieu even though his biological parents might have been Brahmins, or a Brahmin mother originally conceived him. Extending this logic further, no Tīrthaṅkara in the Jain tradition can ever come from an economically weak class. Their financially strong backgrounds also demonstrate their victory in worldly affairs a prerequisite for their later victory in their spiritual careers. Contrariwise, a Brahmin depends on the grace of others for worldly affairs and will depend on the grace of the almighty for spiritual practices. An alternative interpretation for the preference of a Kṣatriya family may be delegitimising the Brahminical authority (Heesterman 1985), especially since the contemporary rituals involved rampant sacrifices of animals, which went against the Jain non-violent tenet (Jaini 1987). The change from Brahmin to Kṣatriya may have been done to ensure Mahāvīra's coronation in the royal lineage.

There is another sectarian dispute about the gender of the 19th Tīrthaṅkara Malli. According to Śvētāmbaras, Malli was the only female Tīrthaṅkara among the twenty-four

Tīrthaṅkaras. However, according to Digambaras, Malli and all the other twenty-three Tīrthaṅkaras are males since liberation is possible only in a male form. Again, this may indicate the gender transformation required for liberation through the Jain practice of penance. The importance of masculinity can be interpreted to highlight that any biological sex must adopt a masculine gender to conquer oneself for Jain liberation. Masculinity is equated with the martial vigour expected and required of males. A feminine surrender is preferred in practices that depend on the grace of the almighty, e.g. in the devotional traditions of Hinduism. However, as exemplified by its Jinas, the victors, the Jain tradition depends solely on one's ultimate austerities that make the feminine gender ineligible for liberation, irrespective of the biological sex. Although today, in the second decade of the twenty-first century, gender transformation surgeries and hormonal changes are becoming increasingly commonplace. The nineteenth-century Indian spiritual master Ramakrishna manifested gender transformation by adopting the role of a feminine devotee in a specific branch of Hindu devotion.[6] Just as Ramakrishna displayed feminine behaviour from a biologically male body, Malli, the nineteenth Jain Tīrthaṅkara, may have displayed masculine features from his female body.

Out of compassion for his mother, Mahāvīra stopped moving inside her womb. Nevertheless, as the mother worried about the fetus's health, he again started making regular movements, allaying her fears. He decided not to renounce his family and worldly life against their wishes.[7] Gods from the heavens showered several kinds of gifts on the earth to celebrate the birth of Mahāvīra: nectar, perfumes, powders, flowers of five distinct colours, gold and jewels.[8] His mother kept him in the womb for nine months and seven and a half days. As the child was born at the most promising astrological position of the planets, the universe celebrated this auspicious event. Eight goddesses from each direction visited the birthplace and celebrated the occasion. Four goddesses from the central celestial region visited and cut the umbilical cord. When the gods carried him to the top of Mount Meru for celebration, Indra became anxious if the baby could withstand the rush of the water and other materials but bowed down to the baby when the baby pushed Meru with his left leg's thumb.[9] The gods filled the royal treasures with precious jewels and wealth and announced that anybody having evil thoughts against the baby or his mother would have their heads cut as a punishment.

After this announcement, the celestial beings celebrated the birth of Mahāvīra once again and then returned.[10] The *Āchārānga Sūtra* (*AS*), one of the primary Śvētāmbara scriptures, vividly describes some of these celebrations. According to the Śvētāmbara text Pauma Chariyam and the Digambara text *Ādipurāṇa,* as cited in Hastīmal (1971: 555), gods started showering wealth six months before the conception of Tīrthaṅkaras. Śvētāmbara Hemachandra's twelfth century Sanskrit text *Triśaṣti Śalākā Puruṣa Caritra* (*TSPC*) and twelfth century Prakrit text *Śrī Mahāvīra Charitam* by a Digambara monk, Guṇachandra, also have similar descriptions of celebrations and the shower of wealth. Some texts mention that the celebrations continued for ten days.

His indifference to worldly affairs was a precursor to his impending renunciatory zeal. He did not insist even on his renunciation and quietly waited for parental permission. However, even as a prince in a royal household, his lifestyle must have remained that of an ascetic, just waiting for the formal initiation. He continued to live a quiet life, as mentioned earlier. His materialistic indifference was evident in his married life and worldly life in general – as if he lived absorbed in his meditation, a soul-oriented lifestyle oblivious of his environment.

BIRTHPLACE[11]

According to some scholars, the Prakrit term in Jain scriptures *Vesāliya,* which means born in Vaiśālī, signifies that Mahāvīra was born in Vaiśālī city of Bihar in north India. According to the Hindu Purāṇas, Vaiśālī was founded by King Viśāla, the son of Ikṣvāku and Alambuṣā. According to the Buddhist texts (Jain 1998), the city was enlarged thrice by combining nearby villages and was named to mean 'large'. Other scholars consider other towns, such as Kundalpur or Kṣatriyakund, his birthplace. The location of Kṣatriyakund is disputed between the Magadh and Videha kingdoms of ancient India. *Āchārānga Sūtra* and *Kalpa Sūtra* (hereafter *KS*) call him a resident of Videha, which spread from Nepal to Northern Bihar (Jain 1998; Mishra 1954). Similarly, Hemachandra's twelfth century Sanskrit text *TSPC* sings the glory of Videha directly and paints it as a spiritual and moral haven (Jain 1998). Although Herman Jacobi (1884: 256) has connected Videha to the region, it may refer to Mahāvīra's excellent physique – *deha* means body in Indian languages. The Bengali translator of *KS*, Basanta Kumar Chattopadhyaya, has also applied this latter interpretation for Videha. The Digambara texts such as *Daśabhakti Ādisangraha* and *Nirvaṇa Bhakti* by Pūjyapāda (CE 464–524), *Harivaṃśa Purāṇa* (1.2.251-2) by Jinasena (*c.* ninth century CE), and *Uttar Purāṇa* by Guṇabhadra (*c.* ninth century CE) consider Kundalpur and Kṣatriyakund to be inside Videha (Jain 1998). According to Kalyāṇa Vijayji, Kundpur was a suburb of Vaiśālī, while Vijayendrasuri has considered both as separate cities. According to *Bhagavati Sūtra*'s ninth chapter, Kṣatriyakund was west of Brāhmaṇkunda, with a large temple in between. Some scholars note that Kṣatriyakund is not mentioned in Jain texts. *Āvaśyaka Niryukti,* hereafter *AN* (394.180), mentions Kundpur and Kundagrām, and *AS* mentions Kṣatriyakund. Kundpur's northern part is Kṣatriyakund, and the southern part is Brāhmaṇkunda, as mentioned in *AS* Chapter

15. Kṣatriyakund had the Kṣatriya clan called Jñātra, mentioned as Jñātik or Nñātik in the Buddhist texts, and the village was also called Jñātragrām. According to the distinguished Hindi author Rāhula Sānkṛtyāyana, Mahāvīra was born in the Jñātra lineage. As mentioned in *Sino-Indian Studies* (1.4.145),[12] Jñātragrām was about 1.5 miles from Vaiśālī. Today, Vaiśālī is in the Tirhut Division of Bihar, where Vasukund near Basārh is considered the location of ancient Kundpur. Based on all the available information, Mahāvīra was born at Kuṇdpur (Kṣatriyakund) in Vaiśālī. He also spent twelve rainy seasons here, as mentioned in the *KS*. The Buddha also spent one rainy season here, allowing women in his congregation in this city (Jain 1945: 12).

PARENTS

As mentioned earlier, Mahāvīra's father was Siddhārtha, and his mother was Triśalā.[13] Jacobi considers Siddhārtha a clan leader, not an emperor, which does not match the textual references in which Siddhārtha is referred to as a king. For instance, *KS* calls him *Rāyā,* i.e. Rājā or king. Guṇachandra's Mahāvīra Charitam (twelfth century.) refers to him as *Narendra,* i.e. king of men, decorated with crown and ornaments. The texts also mention the presence of other leaders of the republics, further showing him to be a king, not merely a clan leader. Jacobi hesitates to accept Siddhārtha as a king due to his less prominence or power than other contemporary kings such as Chetak, who is referred to as the brother of Triśalā in different texts. The fact that she was married to Siddhārtha also demonstrates that both families must be equivalent in status and be royal families, as mentioned in *Mahāvīra Charitam*, *TSPC*, and *Daśabhaktyādisangraha*, for instance. Siddhārtha is mentioned to be in the Ikṣvāku dynasty with Kāśyapa lineage, and Triśalā's lineage is Vāsiṣṭha. In *KS* (105-6), the former is also called Śreyānsa and Yaśasvī, and the latter is also called Videhadinnā and Priyakāriṇī. Videhadinnā refers to her being the sister of Chetak.

ADOLESCENCE

His parents employed five nannies to feed, bathe, decorate, play with, and take care of the child, and the child developed into a young man who enjoyed five kinds of pleasures in taste, touch, smell, sight and hearing, as mentioned in *AS* (2.15). A few commentators have noted two events out of his less eventful adolescent life: his encounter with a snake and an elephant. Although he was hailed as a courageous hero as he tamed both, all such epithets were applied before his renunciation from worldly life. After his renunciation and especially his omniscience, such mundane materialistic 'victories' have little significance compared to his ultimate victory of conquering passions and other tendencies and attributes (Bharill 1976). Once, a heavenly being wanted to test the strength of Vardhamāna, so he suddenly appeared in the play area where Vardhamāna and his friends were playing. While other children ran away from the snake, Vardhamāna humbled him by trouncing on its hood. The serpent quickly appeared as the Sangam Deva and asked for forgiveness from whom he called Mahāvīra, the great valiant hero. In another event, another disguised celestial being is similarly humbled by Vardhamāna. Such events popularised the name Mahāvīra everywhere.

His parents tried to admit him to a traditional boarding school. Āvaśyaka Cūrṇi (hereafter AC) mentions that Indra, the king of the gods, wanted to demonstrate Mahāvīra's encyclopedic knowledge, so asks him questions related to grammar in the presence of his future teacher. As everyone is amazed by Mahāvīra's answers, Indra edits them, and that text is called Aindra Vyākaraṇa.[14] Mahāvīra's apparent indifference (or more knowledge than his teachers, as noted by other commentators Jain 1977: 13) led his parents to arrange for homeschooling. They designed a large study hall with several texts and other devices to study various subjects, but he was uninterested (Jain 2009: 87).

MARRIAGE

Another disputed biographical fact in Mahāvīra's life is his marriage and the birth of his child. According to the Śvētāmbaras, he was married with a child before he renounced to become a wandering monk. However, the Digambaras reject his marriage and child, although some Śvētāmbara texts describe him as unmarried. Some Digambara texts, such as *Harivaṃśa Purāṇa* (by Jinasena in the eighth century), mention that wedding preparations were in progress just before Mahāvīra renounced the worldly life. Both sects refer to the five of the twenty-four Tīrthaṅkaras, Vāsupūjya, Malli, Nemi, Pārśva and Mahāvīra, as Kumāra Pravrajita. However, Digambaras have interpreted Kumāra to mean unmarried, but Śvētāmbaras argue that Kumāra means young prince in many dictionaries. Therefore, they may be married princes, not necessarily unmarried ones as Digambaras argue, before they renounced their worldly lives (Hastīmal 1971: 565)

Another hermeneutic exercise may be necessary to interpret this anomaly. As widely known, Christ was born of a Virgin mother, i.e. a messianic personality such as Jesus Christ demonstrating utmost compassion and kindness needs the mother that remains a virgin even after giving birth to a child. Can Mahāvīra similarly remain unmarried, at least in spirit, although he became a husband and a father? Digambaras caught his untouched pure spirit and declared him to have remained unmarried, while Śvētāmbaras went by the historical fact and declared him to have become a husband and father. Just as somebody can demonstrate the traits of a married life without getting married, Mahāvīra remained psychologically unmarried even after becoming a husband and a father. He remained an independent and fulfilled person and did not depend on anybody else to make him complete. He neither expressed any interest in getting married nor refused to. Moreover, he must be determined to obtain liberation, obviating his desire to marry or carry on his name through his child.

NOTES

1. According to *Āvaśyaka Niryukti* 17: 241 and *Āvaśyaka Cūrṇi* 17: 217, as cited in Hastīmal (1971). Dundas (2020) however assigns 482 BCE as the birthyear of Mahāvīra with continued lack of evidence for any date.
2. As I noted in my earlier monograph (Jain 2023: 5), 'Despite this centuries-old self-conscious Jain identity, Jainism became a separate religion officially with the British census in 1881 (Flügel 2006, 313) and a 'minority religion' in 2014 when the then Indian government, led by the Congress party, accorded the minority status to the Jain community. However, the Hindu Code bills continue to apply to Jains (with Buddhists and Sikhs) for various matters such as inheritance and marriage (Flügel 2005).
3. According to some texts, parents of Mahāvīra were also Pārśva's followers. Even Siddhārtha Gautama followed Pārśva for some time before choosing 'the middle way'.
4. As mentioned in a twelfth century Prakrit text *Śrī Mahāvīra Charitam* by a Digambara monk Guṇachandra, as cited by Hastīmal (1971). Also, mentioned in *Kalpa Sūtra*, 103.
5. There were sixteen dreams according to the Digambara sect but fourteen according to the Śvētāmbara sect.
6. https://www.indica.today/research/conference/spiritual-realization-through-the-performance-of-the-feminine-sri-ramakrishnas-raganuga-bhakti-sadhana-as-a-case-study/ (accessed on 1 May 2023).

7. According to the Śvētāmbara text *Kalpa Sūtra*'s verse ninety-one, as cited in Hastīmal (1971: 551)
8. According to Hemachandra's twelfth century Sanskrit text *Triśaṣti Śalākā Puruṣa Caritra* (10.2.60-4), as cited in Hastīmal (1971: 551).
9. Ibid. (1971: 554).
10. According to Amolak Ṛṣi's *Jambudvīpa Prajñapt*, as cited in Hastīmal (1971: 555).
11. https://timesofindia.indiatimes.com/city/patna/row-over-mahaviras-birthplace/articleshow/232215.cms (accessed on 15 July 2023).
12. As cited in Hastīmal (1971: 558) referring to the Buddhist text *Mahāparinirvāṇa Sūtra*'s Chinese edition.
13. Dundas (2020: 124) spells the mother's name as Tiśalā or Tisalā. All the Jain texts that I have referred never use this spelling.

CHAPTER 2

Dīkṣā
Renunciation

Mahāvīra's parents followed the teachings of the twenty-third Tīrthaṅkara Pārśva, took the vow of *Sallekhanā* (fast unto death), and passed away when he was twenty-eight. After their death, Mahāvīra could renounce his worldly life, so he asked his brother Nandivardhan about renouncing his worldly life. However, Nandivardhan disapproved of the request (*AS* 2.15) and convinced him to postpone his decision for two more years. Mahāvīra lived with his family for two more years, but his life was now of a celibate renunciant, abandoning unboiled water and food after the sunset. He lived with vows of truth, kindness, and other noble values devoid of anger and other negative attributes. Like an ascetic and unlike a prince, he slept on the ground and meditated most of the time. He donated 10.8 million gold coins daily, totalling 3 billion 942 million annually (*AS* 9.11).

As he spent his next two years and turned thirty, it was finally time for his renunciation. His brother and uncle planned an elaborate farewell ceremony for the great renunciation and ordered 1,008 gold and other coins. On the tenth day of the first month of the Hemant season (early winter), the rite for his renunciation ensued on an auspicious early evening. Mahāvīra fasted for two days and was seated on a special throne facing eastward. He was oil-massaged, bathed, dried, and then sandalwood paste was applied to him. He was adorned in a lightweight, expensive robe and jewellery and seated in a palanquin with horses leading the way and elephants on the left and the right. Riding an elephant, his brother King Nandivardhan followed him with other chariots. The massive procession reached a garden where Mahāvīra got down, removed his clothes and jewellery, and pulled his hair. His hair was immersed in the celestial ocean, while his clothes and jewellery were collected in white cloth. The musical instruments were silenced to maintain complete silence for the occasion. Mahāvīra bowed to the earlier enlightened beings and pledged to renounce three kinds of violent acts – physical, verbal and mental, which was witnessed by the massive crowd assembled to celebrate this extraordinary rite of passage. As a beloved prince of a large republic, like the Buddha, he could have enjoyed a life of abundant luxuries but chose a difficult path of ultimate austerities. He soon moved away from the crowd and took another pledge in complete isolation and silence, as recorded in *AS*: 'From twelve and half years from today, until omniscience arises, I will not have any attachment for my body and will withstand everything by any being with equanimity.' He reached the village Kurmārgrām just before sunset and started meditating. Some later commentaries have mentioned him donating half of his cloth out of compassion to an older man on the way; however, no scripture can corroborate this encounter. *AS* and *KS* mention that the *devaduṣya*, an upper garment made of wool, fell off him after thirteen months.

THE FIRST DAY AS AN ASCETIC

As Mahāvīra remained Sthāṇu, immovable, standing in meditation outside Kurmārgrām, a herder brought his bulls, left them for grazing there, and went away to a nearby village.

The bulls wandered far away, busy grazing. Later, he returned to collect his bulls and asked Mahāvīra about them. Upon receiving no response from Mahāvīra, the herdsman searched for his bulls the entire night. As he returned to Mahāvīra the following day, he found his bulls, making him suspicious of Mahāvīra's intentions. As the herder raised his hand to attack Mahāvīra, suddenly Indra appeared out of nowhere, protected Mahāvīra, and rebuked the herdsman, as noted in *TSPC*. Indra sought Mahāvīra's permission to protect him from any potential threats. However, Mahāvīra asserted that Jinas accomplish their omniscience and enlightenment based on their penance without taking help from anybody. Still, *TSPC* mentions that Indra appointed Siddhārtha, a celestial being for Mahāvīra's protection, bowed to Mahāvīra and left.

The next day, Mahāvīra visited Kollāga, where he broke his six-day fast by accepting porridge, made from sugar and ghee, from a Brahmin named Bahul. Texts describe the event as a celebration by gods showering five kinds of precious gems. While Digambaras insisted on his complete nudity from his very first day of renunciation, the Śvētāmbaras insisted that he had a divine piece of cloth covering his body. Perhaps both sects hold some truth in that he was naked, but nobody noticed his innocent and natural appearance. His spiritual brilliance overshadowed his physical state as if a special cloth gifted by gods covered him. His upper garment, *devaduṣya*, fell off after thirteen months, as mentioned in *KS* and *AS*, and then he practised complete nudity for over four decades until his death and *mokṣa*.

As a wandering ascetic, he used to stay at randomly found abandoned cottages, rest areas, or water stations. He would not protect his body even in the extreme cold by covering his arms. He kept wandering around with open arms, literally and figuratively, even as other renunciants tried to shelter around warmer places or covered with woollen garments during winter. In addition to extreme cold and heat, he withstood bites from reptiles or insects, other skin issues and injuries, and even bird bites on his naked body. Sometimes, people used to attack, beat, or insult him, assuming he was a thief, and elsewhere, women tried to lure him.

However, against all odds, he remained steadfast in his penance every moment. He would immediately vacate a place if anyone any where told him to do so. He rarely slept in his penance years and would start walking at night to prevent drowsiness. While walking, he would not glance anywhere, turn back, or talk to anyone. He would accept only residual vegetarian food without expecting any special delicacies. He went for alms collection to anybody without discrimination against rich or poor. His detachment from his body was remarkable. In addition to handling heat and cold calmly, he would not take any medicine for any disease, react if something fell in his eyes, or scratch for itching. During his renunciation ceremony, aromatic ointments and oils were applied to his body, which attracted insects that kept sucking the blood out of his body. Still, he remained unaffected by all pain or suffering.

THE FIRST YEAR OF PENANCE

From Kollāga, he went to Morāka, where Duijjantak, the head of a monastery, was a friend of Mahāvīra's father, King Siddhārtha. According to *TSPC*, Mahāvīra accepted Duijjantak's invitation, stayed for a night there, and the next day before leaving, accepted the invitation to return for the rainy season. After wandering in nearby villages, he returned to Duijjantak's monastery and stayed in a leafy cottage during the rainy season. That region faced a severe drought, drying up all grass and other plants, so the nearby cattle started grazing upon Mahāvīra's cottage's tree leaves. When other residents complained to the head against Mahāvīra for not protecting his cottage, the head asked Mahāvīra sarcastically, 'Why you cannot protect your dwelling being a Kṣatriya prince when even birds can do that easily?' Mahāvīra realised that his stay there was inconveniencing other residents, and the cottage was merely an excuse to express it. He became a renunciant not to protect any dwelling at the cost of troubling other living beings, especially in an emergency like famine. Therefore, he left that monastery after fifteen days of stay there with the five vows, as reported in *KS* (although not mentioned in the original scriptures): First, not to stay in an unpleasant space. Second, meditate the entire time. Third, maintain silence and avoid conversing with anyone. Fourth, eat by hand without using any utensils. Fifth, do not interact with any householders. According to *AS*, he never accepted food in a utensil. However, other commentaries mention that he used a utensil before taking these five vows.

From the monastery, he walked towards Asthigrām and reached there by the evening, where he found a lonely place outside the village. He settled there in a corner, ignoring the villagers' warning that an evil spirit, Shūlapāṇī, resided there. As recorded in *TSPC*, Mahāvīra embraced such challenges, faced them with open arms, and reformed the violent people causing such challenges. In the evening, the priest Indra Sharma visited the place, and after performing rituals, he asked everybody to leave, including Mahāvīra. However, Mahāvīra kept silently meditating, and the priest left. Shūlapāṇī appeared in the dark, noticed Mahāvīra there, and thundered furiously, shaking the entire region. Like an elephant, he trounced Mahāvīra with his legs and bit Mahāvīra with his teeth. Like a demon, he pierced Mahāvīra with his sharp nails and teeth. As mentioned in some commentaries, he caused such extreme pain in Mahāvīra's ears, eyes, nose, head, teeth, back and nails that an ordinary human would have died. Still, Mahāvīra remained stable in his meditation, enduring all the assaults. According to *TSPC*, by the night's end, Shūlapāṇī fell on Mahāvīra's feet and left after asking for forgiveness.

With just one *muhurta* (48 minutes) left for the night, Mahāvīra fell asleep momentarily while standing in meditation. As commentators note, he saw ten dreams in his sleep: First, defeating a demon spirit. Second, a white male cuckoo appeared in his service. Third, another multicoloured male cuckoo appeared. Fourth, a pair of glittering jewel garlands. Fifth, a white group of cattle. Sixth, a pond with full-bloom lotus. Seventh, swimming across a vast ocean. Eighth, the sun, with its infinite rays, illuminating the world. Ninth, his intestines encircled Mount Mānuṣottara. Tenth, climbing Mount Meru. He immediately woke up after these ten dreams, this being the last time he slept in his life. He remained vigilant in his meditation and never slept after that. An astrologer, Utpal, lived in that village. Utpal was an ascetic in Pārśva's lineage but later switched to a householder's life. As he heard about Mahāvīra's night stay in the spirit-infested place outside his village, anxious Utpal rushed there in the morning. He was astonished and joyous as he found Mahāvīra immersed in his meditation. Later, he explained Mahāvīra's ten dreams. First, Mahāvīra defeating the spirit referred to getting rid of delusionary *karma*. Second, seeing a white cuckoo meant obtaining the highest bright meditative stage. Third, seeing a multicoloured male cuckoo implied his preaching of various kinds of knowledge. Utpal could not interpret the fourth, so Mahāvīra interpreted that he would preach both for ascetics and householders. Fifth, white cattle suggested that he would establish the white-clad congregation. Sixth, the lotus pond indicated gods serving him. Seventh, crossing the ocean specified his transcending the world and achieving ultimate liberation. Eighth, the radiating sun denoted his achieving omniscience. Ninth, his intestines covering the world conveyed his worldwide reputation. Tenth, climbing Mount Meru construed his universal preaching as a spiritual authority. For the rest of his first rainy season at Asthigrām, he did not encounter any other trouble and completed eight series of fasts of fifteen days each.

THE SECOND YEAR OF PENANCE

After completing the rainy season at Asthigrām, he arrived at Morāka and stayed at a park. As mentioned in the commentaries, the celestial being Siddhārtha accompanied Mahāvīra everywhere. In Morāka, he glorified Mahāvīra as a knower of the past, present, and future, and people started flocking to Mahāvīra for this purpose. However, Mahāvīra was deeply meditating; therefore, Siddhārtha started sharing astrological forecasts of the people, one of whom cited the name of Achchhandak as another good astrologer. When Siddhārtha exposed the sins committed by Achchhandak, people investigated them and found them accurate. Therefore, Achchhandak's influence waned from the people, and people started coming to Mahāvīra. However, when Achchhandak begged Mahāvīra not to hurt his livelihood, Mahāvīra agreed to move away from Morāka and walked towards Northern Vāchālā (*AC* 277). Vāchālā was divided into North and South by two rivers, Sūvarṇakūlā and Rūpakūlā. His *devaduṣya*, the upper garment, fell off from his shoulder near Sūvarṇakūlā's bank and was stuck in a thorny bush. He ensured that the garment was reachable by his followers and remained naked for his entire life. According to *AC* 277, a Brahmin followed Mahāvīra, grabbed his garment, and returned home.

Chandakauśika

While walking from Morāka to North Vāchālā, Mahāvīra reached another monastery, Kanakhamal. There were two ways from there to Vāchālā, one from within the monastery and the other around it. He chose the latter and met some cattle herders on the way. They warned him about a venomous snake, Chandakauśika, in the area and suggested he choose the alternative path. Mahāvīra ignored their advice and silently walked ahead, determined to reform the snake.

Chandakauśika was an ascetic in his previous life. While begging for alms once, he accidentally trounced and killed a frog under his feet. When his disciple told him about it, he showed another dead frog nearby as an excuse. When his guru did not repent for this accident during the evening ritual, the disciple reminded him a few times to no avail. The angry guru rose to beat the disciple but hit a pillar and died. He was reborn as a celestial being, and in the next life, he was born into the family of the head of the Kanakhamal monastery, having five hundred ascetics. The baby was named Kauśika, but to keep his name different from other people with the same name, he was renamed Chandakauśika. He became the head of the monastery in time. He became too attached to the forest of the monastery to let anybody else take fruit from there. People left the place, and he would beat any cattle herder passing by the area. Once, a few princes from Seyaviya came and destroyed the forest. When Chandakauśika returned, he learned of this destruction from others, and he furiously attacked the princes with an axe, who quickly ran away. Blinded in rage, he fell into a pit, and the axe fell on his head. After his death, he was reborn as a snake in the same forest. Continuing the anger and attachment from his previous life, he prohibited anyone from entering the forest. Many ascetics also left the monastery. He poisoned and killed even birds in the forest.

Mahāvīra entered the forest and started meditating with waves of benevolence flowing from him for all. As soon as Chandakauśika saw Mahāvīra standing in his territory, he furiously hissed with fatal venom but could not affect Mahāvīra's meditation. He then ferociously attacked Mahāvīra and bit him with lethal poison. However, the snake was shocked to see milk instead of blood coming from Mahāvīra's body. Commentators have interpreted this incident by comparing Mahāvīra's benevolence with motherly love for her child, transforming her blood into her milk. Astonished with Mahāvīra's universal selfless love and compassion, the snake finally calmed down. When Mahāvīra came out of his meditation, he blessed the snake and reminded him of his violent acts in past lives that led to his birth as a snake. More violence as a snake would ensure his falling into even lower life forms, so he must act now and choose non-violence to improve his present and future lives. According to *AN* (467), the snake was suddenly awakened and regretted the violence in his past lives. Thus, Mahāvīra's ultimate penance cooled down even the fiery snake, who vowed never to hurt anyone. Mahāvīra blessed him and moved on, but the snake's life was changed forever as he became a harmless, non-violent creature. As people started revering this renewed snake with milk, ants started crawling on him, and eventually, the snake succumbed to their bites and passed away. Thus, the snake completed his life with auspicious actions and attained eighth heaven (*AC* 1.273). In this way, the snake Chandakauśika's non-violence was karmically rewarded and paved his way to a higher goal of ultimate liberation.

The Boat Ride

After liberating the snake Chandakauśika, Mahāvīra arrived at North Vāchālā, where he broke his fifteen-day fast with rice pudding at Nāgasena's house. From here, he walked towards Śvetāmbikā, whose king Pradeśī welcomed him with open arms. From here, he moved towards Surabhipur and had to cross the river Ganges in a boat. As the boat departed, an owl hooted from the right-hand side. An astrologer riding in the boat explained that an impending threat would be thwarted by the presence of the great soul on the boat (*AC* 280). The boat soon found itself engulfed in a powerful storm caused by an evil spirit trying to take revenge on Mahāvīra from a previous life. As usual, Mahāvīra kept calm, the storm subsided, and the boat safely reached the other bank with help from two youths, Kambal and Śambal. An astrologer named Puṣya was astonished to note that somebody destined to be an emperor was standing naked in meditation on the banks of the river Ganges. As he was about to throw his Sanskrit texts into the river, a celestial being revealed the real identity of Mahāvīra (*AC* 1.282).

Makkhali Gośāla

While continuing his wanderings across northern India, he arrived at Nālandā, a suburb of Rājgira in present-day Bihar, for his second rainy season retreat. Makkhali Gośāla also arrived there and was impressed with Mahāvīra's penance of one month-long fast. The fast-breaking ceremony was held at the home of a merchant Vijay. Similarly, the second month-long fast-breaking ceremony was at Anand's home, and the third was at Sunand's (*BS* 15.451, 1214). As the entire town of Rājgira admired the great ascetic Mahāvīra and his hosts, Makkhali Gośāla approached Mahāvīra and requested him to make some predictions. Mahāvīra told him to expect stale rice, sour buttermilk, and fake money in alms. Gośāla failed to collect alms in wealthy communities and received stale rice, sour buttermilk, and fake currency at an ironsmith's home, as Mahāvīra had predicted, and mentioned in *TSPC* 10.3.393, but not in any other primary text. Gośāla accepted fatalism as an authentic philosophy after this event. As the four-month rainy season ended, Mahāvīra concluded his fourth and final month-long fast by moving from Nālandā to Kollāga at Bahul Brahmin's home. Gośāla searched for Mahāvīra and was again impressed by his excellent reputation at the new location of Kollāga. According to *BS* 15.1 and *TSPC* 10.3., Gośāla persuades Mahāvīra to accept him as his disciple, to which Mahāvīra obliges. Gośāla follows his guru, Mahāvīra, for the next six years.

THE THIRD YEAR OF PENANCE

From Kollāga, Mahāvīra with Gośāla arrived at Svarṇakhal (a town in present-day West Bengal). On their way, Gośāla was tempted by villagers preparing rice pudding, but Mahāvīra predicted that the breaking of the cooking pan would ruin the pudding. Gośāla ignored the prediction and waited for the pudding while Mahāvīra moved on further. However, Mahāvīra's prediction again turned out to be accurate, convincing Gośāla once again with the fatalism ideology. Later, they reached Brāhmaṇgāon, a village in the Munshiganj district of present-day Bangladesh divided into Nandapāṭaka and Upanandapāṭaka. Mahāvīra received yoghurt-mixed rice at Nand's home in the former, while Gośāla received stale rice at Upananda's home. When Gośāla refused this food, the maid threw it on his head. Angry Gośāla cursed the donor and left. According to *AC* 1.284, the nearby celestial beings burned Upananda's home to prove his curse right. Afterwards, Mahāvīra arrived at Champā in the Anga kingdom in present-day Bihar, where he completed his third rainy season practising different postures and meditation. He kept two two-month-long fasts in the four months of the rainy season. After the first two months, the fast-breaking ceremony was held inside Champā and the ceremony after the second fast was held outside Champā (*AC* 1.284).

THE FOURTH YEAR OF PENANCE

From Champā, he arrived at Kālāya with Gośāla and stayed at an abandoned house. While Mahāvīra meditated, Gośāla hid behind a door and tried gossiping with the maid Vidyunmati. When she complained to the village head, his son Puruṣsingh beat Gośāla. From there, both visited Pattakālaya, where Mahāvīra meditated at another lonely place, but Gośāla again invited people's anger due to his misbehaviour. From Pattakālaya, he went to Kumāraka (*AC* 1.285) and resumed his meditation in the Champagaramaṇīya Park. An ascetic leader, Munichandra, in the lineage of the 23rd Tīrthaṅkara Pārśva, stayed with his disciples nearby. He appointed one of his disciples as the congregation's leader and adopted a fully naked ascetic lifestyle. Gośāla requested Mahāvīra to join him for the alms collection but went alone. Gośāla encountered Munichandra's disciples and ridiculed them for their colourful robes and possessions. When Gośāla tried to project his guru Mahāvīra as a superior ascetic, he received similar ridicule back. Angry Gośāla cursed their dwelling place to burn away. When the place's owner, a potter named Kūpanaya, returned, he saw Munichandra standing in meditation outside. The drunkard potter assumed Munichandra to be a thief and tried killing him, but Munichandra continued his meditation, achieved omniscience, and passed away (*AC* 1.286) (*TSPC* 10.3.470-7).

Later, Mahāvīra reached Chorāka (the present-day town of Chauri Chaura in Gorakhpur district in Uttar Pradesh), notorious for thieves. At the town entrance, the security guard enquired about his identity. However, Mahāvīra continued his meditative silence and did not respond. The guards assumed he was a criminal or spy and imprisoned and tortured him. Astrologer Utpal's sisters – Soma and Jayanti – heard the news and asked the guards to release Mahāvīra. Realising their mistake, the guards asked for forgiveness and freed him. Later, Mahāvīra moved to Pṛṣṭhachampā, where he spent his fourth rainy season retreat in a four-month-long fast.

THE FIFTH YEAR OF PENANCE

Later, Mahāvīra reached Kayaṅgalā (*AC* 288), where he started meditating at a place owned by a heretic, Dariddathera. Then, he moved to Sāvatthī, where he meditated outside the town despite the severe chilly weather, while Gośāla suffered the entire night. Nearby, people were busy singing and dancing, celebrating a religious festival. When Gośāla ridiculed the celebration, people threw him out, beating him multiple times. After learning that he was Mahāvīra's disciple, they ignored him, and the elders kept playing their musical instruments louder. In the morning, Mahāvīra reached Śrāvastī, where the wife of Pitṛadatta prepared a pudding with meat and donated it to Gośāla as part of a ritual for her son's protection. This event was also predicted correctly, further convincing Gośāla of fatalism.

Then, Mahāvīra reached Haledug village with a nearby large Haledug tree, where he decided to stay for a night. Other travellers also stayed there at night and burned some sticks for heat on a wintry night. The morning after they left, the fire suddenly spread near Mahāvīra's feet, but his meditation continued even as his feet burned (*AC* 288). After completing his meditation in the afternoon, he arrived at Āvarta via Nāngalā, where he meditated at a Baldeva temple. Gośāla received more beatings due to his habit of scaring children. From Āvarta, after walking across many other villages, Mahāvīra reached Chorāka. Once again, after Gośāla was beaten, he cursed to burn the place. Then, Mahāvīra arrived at Kalambukā, where the two brothers –Megh and Kalahasti – ruled the nearby hill region.. Mahāvīra kept silent when asked about his identity and was beaten by Kālhastī. Megh, however, remembered Mahāvīra from their meeting a few years ago in Kundagrām and apologised for his brother's cruelty (*AC* 290).

After this incident, Mahāvīra moved away from familiar regions, where he could quickly cleanse his past *karma* without any protection from strangers. He entered Lādh (or Rādh), divided by the Ajay River, whose northern region was Vajra and southern Shubhra (*AC* 287). According to *AS* 9.3, pp. 83-92, he did not get a dwelling place or appropriate food, and stray dogs used to attack him. However, without malice for anybody, he kept wandering the region calmly, even amidst violent attacks by locals. While moving towards the Malaya region, he was lethally attacked by two smugglers who treated him like a bad omen (*AC* 1.290).

THE SIXTH YEAR OF PENANCE

His next rainy season retreat happened at Bhaddilā, where he held a four-month-long fast culminating at Kadali Samāgam and Jambu Sand. Here, the locals insulted Gośāla yet again. Then, Mahāvīra visited Tambāya, where a senior ascetic Nandiṣeṇ was staying with whom Gośāla debated (*AC* 191). Then, Mahāvīra moved to Kūvīya, where he was once again beaten due to a misunderstanding about his identity of being a spy. Two Jain nuns, Vijayā and Pragalbhā, rushed, revealed his real identity, and rescued him (*AC* 292). The locals realised their mistake and apologised. Then, Mahāvīra started walking towards Vaiśālī, while Gośāla travelled towards Rājgira lamenting that Mahāvīra did not protect him from all the beatings and insults.

At Vaiśālī, Mahāvīra asked an ironsmith and started meditating at his workshop. One of its workers who had been sick for the last six months suddenly started feeling better and returned to work. However, when he saw Mahāvīra meditating there, he tried to hit him with his tool (*AC* 292) but could not hurt him. Afterwards, Mahāvīra moved to Grāmk, where he meditated at Vibhelak Yakṣa's place. Then, he visited Śāli Śīrṣa's garden in the severe winter of January, where an evil woman, Katapūtanā, tried to torture him by spraying freezing water on his body. He withstood this attack with equanimity, achieved the next level of spiritual advancement, and Katapūtanā left after asking for forgiveness (*AC* 293). Then, he moved on to Bhadrikā, 8 kilometres south of the present-day city of Bhagalpur in Bihar, where he spent his sixth rainy season retreat with a four-month-long fast. After wandering separately for six months, Gośāla joined him again here. According to *AC* 293, both moved to Magadh from here.

THE SEVENTH YEAR OF PENANCE

After visiting several places in Magadh for trouble-free eight months, Mahāvīra stayed at Ālambhiyā for his seventh four-month rainy season retreat in which he kept the four-month-long fast. The fast culmination ceremony happened outside the town, after which he moved to Kandāg and Bhaddaṇā, where he stayed at Vāsudeva and Baladeva temples, respectively. Gośāla disparaged the deity images, so he was beaten again. From Bhaddaṇā, Mahāvīra went to Bahusāl and meditated in the Sāl (*Shorea robusta*) forest outside the town. Here, another female, Shālārya, tried to trouble him but apologised later as he remained unperturbed.

THE EIGHTH YEAR OF PENANCE

From Bhaddaṇā, he reached Lohārgalā, but continuing his vow of silence, he did not respond to the security guard's questions about his identity. The guard apprehended him in the court of King Jitaśatru, but when a local recognised him, the king respected him and bid farewell for his onward journey (*AC* 294). Then, he walked towards Purimtāla, near the present-day city of Prayag in Uttar Pradesh, where he meditated in the

Śakatmukh garden. Then, he moved on to Unnāg, Gaubhūmi, and Rājgira. He completed his eighth year with another four-month fast in Rājgira during the rainy season retreat, culminating outside the town.

THE NINTH YEAR OF PENANCE

He completed his ninth year with his rainy season retreat in a completely unknown territory, welcoming extreme tortures and insults to cleanse his past karma from his soul (*AC* 294).

THE TENTH YEAR OF PENANCE

As he was walking from Siddhārthapur to Kurmārgrām, his companion Gośāla noticed a sesame plant with seven flowers and asked him if this plant would produce fruits. When Mahāvīra forecasted in the affirmative, Gośāla destroyed the plant to prove the forecast wrong. According to *AC* 297, the sudden downpour fixed the plant in the soil again. Then, he arrived at Kurmārgrām, where an ascetic named Vaiśyāyan was in a yoga posture focusing on the sun. Gośāla angered him by commenting on his long-braided hair, so the ascetic attacked him. When the ascetic realised that Gośāla was Mahāvīra's disciple, he forgave Gośāla and asked for forgiveness from Mahāvīra. After some time, Mahāvīra walked again towards Siddhārthapur. On the way, Gośāla remembered the sesame plant prediction and asked Mahāvīra about it. Mahāvīra again showed him the plant that flourished even after Gośāla tried to uproot it. After this incident, Gośāla decided to stop following Mahāvīra and started thinking about propounding his ideology separately.

Later, Mahāvīra came to Vaiśālī, where some young boys ill-treated him, but his father's friend, King Śankha, came to rescue him and bowed down to him (*AC* 299). Then, Mahāvīra walked towards Vāṇiyagrām after crossing the river Gandaki, for which he could not pay the boatman. The angry boatman tried to punish him, but King Śankha's son Chitra appeared at the right time and saved Mahāvīra (*AC* 299). At Vāṇiyagrām, Mahāvīra met Anand, a disciple in the lineage of the 23rd Tīrthaṅkara Pārśvanātha, who bowed to Mahāvīra and predicted that Mahāvīra would soon attain omniscience based on his strong willpower and perseverance amid extreme torments. From there, Mahāvīra moved to Sāvatthī, where he completed his tenth rainy season retreat with another long fast (*AC* 300).

THE ELEVENTH YEAR OF PENANCE

For his eleventh year, he moved to Sānulatthiya, where he fasted for sixteen days. He broke his fast by accepting leftover food from a maidservant, who was rewarded appropriately for her kindness and respect for Mahāvīra and was freed from her servitude. Then, Mahāvīra moved to Dṛdhabhūmi and started meditating in a garden outside the town. Sangam Deva tried to disturb his meditation in twenty different ways in one night: by showering sand, throwing ants, throwing mosquitoes, throwing termites, throwing scorpions, throwing mongooses, throwing snakes, throwing mice, forcing elephants, throwing spears, forcing tigers, wailing like his parents, burning fire under his feet, forcing birds, forcing thunderstorms, forcing winds, burying in the soil, appearing like a god, appearing like a nymph. Sangam even tried to scare Mahāvīra by assembling five hundred thieves against him. Mahāvīra completed his meditation with equanimity and moved to Balukā, Suyog, Suchchhetā, Malabh, and Hastiśirṣa (*AC* 311), where Sangam tried but failed to trouble Mahāvīra. He even broke into some homes disguised as a burglar, but when caught, blamed his 'guru', Mahāvīra, who was meditating in a garden at the Tosli village. As people rushed to attack Mahāvīra, Mahābhūti appeared and told the villagers about his identity.

Mahāvīra then reached the Mosali village, where Sangam again conspired to accuse him of theft. Fortunately, a local administrator, Sumāgadh, recognised and rescued him. Then, Mahāvīra reached Tosali, where he meditated outside the village. Here, Sangam accumulated several weapons around him in a new conspiracy and, when caught for another stealing attempt, tried to blame Mahāvīra. The local administrators sentenced Mahāvīra to be hung, but the noose around his neck broke seven times, and Mahāvīra was freed (*AC* 313). Then, Mahāvīra reached Siddhārthapur, where Sangam's yet another false allegation was proved false with timely help by a horse trader named Kauśik (*AC* 313). Then, Mahāvīra reached the Vajra village, where people had cooked rice porridge for a celebration, but Sangam ensured that Mahāvīra did not get any food in alms. After six months of harassment attempts, Sangam finally gave up and apologised. Without any malice, Mahāvīra revisited the same village and broke his six-month fast by accepting food from an old lady, Vassapālak. From here, he visited Ālambhiyā, Śvetāmbikā, Sāvatthī, Kauśāmbī, Vārāṇasī, Rājgira, Mithilā, and finally, Vaiśālī, where he completed his eleventh rainy season retreat with another four-month-long fast at the local Baladeva temple in a garden outside the town. At the end of his eleventh rainy season fast, Mahāvīra accepted food from a wealthy local family. At the same time, another wealthy-turned-poor person waited to feed him for four months and was rewarded for his patience with the next birth in heaven.

THE TWELFTH YEAR OF PENANCE

He started his twelfth year at Sunsumār, where he was predicted to attain omniscience soon. According to *BS* 145: 302, he meditated under the Ashoka tree (*Saraca indica*). From here, he visited Bhogpur, Nandigrām, and Medhiyāgrām, where cattle herders tried to trouble him. Then, he moved to Kauśāmbī and pledged to accept food only after the time of almsgiving from an enslaved, chained, shaved-head, tear-eyed princess who could offer *urad* beans (*Vigna mungo* or black gram) while standing on her house's threshold having kept a fast for three days. Since such a rare condition was rare to be fulfilled, he continued his fast for four months without accepting food from anyone. Once, he visited the house of Sugupta, a local minister in the royal court. Sugupta's wife Nanda tried to offer alms to Mahāvīra, but keeping his secret pledge, he did not accept anything. A royal maidservant, Vijayā, noticed the concern of Nanda and Sugupta. She shared it with Queen Mṛgāvatī, who shared it with her husband King Shatānīka, who in turn announced Mahāvīra's ongoing fast and relevant rules for almsgiving to Jain ascetics within the entire kingdom, but nobody could give alms due to his difficult pledge. After completing five months and twenty-five days of his fast, Mahāvīra visited the house of a wealthy businessman named Dhannā. There, he found Princess Chandanā, fasting for the last three days, waiting with *urad* beans for Dhannā. Dhannā's wife had kept Chandanā chained and even shaved her head. Chandanā was delighted that Mahāvīra visited their house, but she cried when he declined the alms because one condition was still unfulfilled. As soon as Mahāvīra saw her tears, all the conditions of his pledge were met, and he finally accepted alms. Mahāvīra later accepted her as his first female disciple, who led a massive congregation of 36,000 nuns.

From Kauśāmbī, he moved to Sumangal, Suchhettā, Pālak, and Champānagarī. At Champānagarī, he completed his fast for four months in the rainy season retreat and thus completed his twelfth year. Here, a Brahmin Swātidatta hosted him and asked many philosophical questions related to the soul and the soul's attributes (*AC* 320). From here, he moved to Jambhiyagrām,

Medhiyāgrām, and Chhamāṇigrām (*AC* 321). He meditated outside Chhamāṇigrām, where a herder left his grazing bulls around him. After he returned to pick his bulls, he asked Mahāvīra about their whereabouts, but Mahāvīra kept silent. The angry herder picked up some sticks and hammered them in Mahāvīra's ears, but Mahāvīra withstood even this extreme pain calmly. Then, he moved to Madhyama Pāvā and visited a merchant named Siddhārtha for alms. Siddhārtha conversed with his doctor friend Kharak, who quickly realised Mahāvīra was suffering from something sharp piercing him. Since Mahāvīra did not stop for any treatment, Siddhārtha and his doctor friend Kharak both visited the park where Mahāvīra was meditating. They massaged his body, removed the sticks from his ears, and applied medicine for healing. Coincidentally, this last attack was the most painful and, like the first, was also by a cattle herder (*KS* 116).

In his twelve years of penance, he fasted most of the time and ate some food – rice, dates, or pulses – on only 349 days out of 4,380 days. His fasts included,

1. One six-month fast
2. One 175-days fast
3. Nine four-month fasts
4. Two three-month fasts
5. Two two-and-a-half-month fasts
6. Six two-month fasts
7. Two one-and-a-half-month fasts
8. Twelve one-month fasts
9. Seventy-two-fortnight fasts
10. One Bhadra-Pratimā fast for two days
11. One Mahābhadra-Pratimā fast for four days
12. One Sarvatobhadra-Pratimā fast for ten days
13. 229 six-day fasts
14. Twelve eight-day fasts

15. 349 days of fast-breaking ceremonies
16. One day of initiation into renunciation.

Various texts use epithets for him, such as detached like a bronze utensil, pure like a conch horn, dynamic like the soul, independent like the sky, free like the wind, clean like autumn water, spotless like a lotus, controlling his senses like a turtle, without attachment or detachment – like a rhinoceros, wandering like a bird, courageous like an elephant, strong like a bull, awe-inspiring like a lion, equanimous like a mountain, solemn like an ocean, soothing like the moon, radiant like the sun, glittering like gold, and scintillating like fire.

CHAPTER 3

Keval Jñāna
Omniscience

He attained *Keval Jñāna*, omniscience, after destroying all his *karmas* in twelve and half years of penance. It was the second month and the fourth fortnight of summer, one afternoon of the tenth day of the Hindu month of Vaiśākh, Mahavira was outside Jambhṛkāgrām, on the banks of Ṛjubālukā River, near a garden, under a Sal tree (*Shorea robusta*) and was in cow-milking yogic posture (*Gauduhasana*). With omniscience, he could see and know the past, present, and future of all beings in the universe – humans, animals, gods, demons, and the rest. According to most accounts, after attaining this supreme knowledge, his first public discourse had no humans in attendance, so nobody pledged to follow him. On the contrary, his twenty-three predecessors had humans in their first public assembly, and many adopted major vows following their preachers.

From here, he moved to Madhyama Pāvā, where Ārya Somil sponsored an extensive ritual with prominent scholars in attendance. Mahāvīra gave his first significant discourse in Pāvāpurī attended by humans and many other species. He sat on a high throne and spoke in the Ardhamagadhi Prakrit language (*AC* 539). When scholars at the nearby ritual noticed some prominent people skipping the ritual to attend Mahāvīra's preaching assembly, they were intrigued and envious. The leading scholar, Indrabhūti, decided to defeat Mahāvīra in a debate, so he visited him with about five hundred other scholars and students. Mahāvīra addressed Indrabhūti by his full name, Indrabhūti Gautama, which further astonished him. Indrabhūti decided to interrogate Mahāvīra to check his omniscience. Mahāvīra understood his confusion about the soul, and Indrabhūti accepted Mahāvīra's detailed explanation. He and five hundred others became Mahāvīra's first disciples at that time. Indrabhūti was later known as Gautama and remained the leading disciple in Mahāvīra's congregation of over 50,000 ascetics.

Afterwards, Agnibhūti and nine other scholars joined the congregation with their disciples. Mahāvīra taught them tripadī, based on which they wrote various Jain scriptures (Twelve 'limbs' and fourteen Pūrvas). They were known as gaṇadharas, i.e. leaders of groups (of disciples). That day, 4,400 people joined Mahāvīra's congregation, including the eleven gaṇadharas. The first five gaṇadharas had five hundred disciples, the sixth and seventh had 350 each, and the eighth, ninth, tenth and eleventh had three hundred each. Chandanā was the first nun, while Śankha Śataka and Sulasā were the first male and female householder disciples. Thus, Mahāvīra was proclaimed tīrthaṅkara having established the Jain congregation with ascetics and householders of all genders on the eleventh day of the Hindu month Vaiśākh in Madhyama Pāvā's Mahāsena forest. He spoke to the congregation. According to the Digambara version of this event, it occurred on the sixty-sixth day after his enlightenment.

THE FIRST YEAR AS THE TĪRTHAṄKARA

From Madhyama Pāvā, with his 4,400 ascetic disciples, he passed through several villages, reached Rājgira, and spent his rainy season retreat at a temple compound outside the town. Rājgira had several householders who were of the previous Tīrthaṅkara Pārśvanātha's lineage. As King Śreṇika heard the news of his arrival, he visited the congregation with his administrators and other staff and bowed down to him. He and his minister Abhaya Kumar became Mahāvīra's householder disciples. Prince Nandiṣeṇa also received permission for renunciation from his parents despite some discouraging warnings against it. Once, he reached a prostitute's house for alms. After much persuasion by her, he agreed to live with her on the condition that he would have his meals only after sending ten people daily for initiation. According to *TSPC*, he could send only nine people one day, so he left the prostitute's home and went for his renunciation again. Thus, he transformed many people and completed his thirteenth rainy season retreat at Rājgira.

THE SECOND YEAR AS THE TĪRTHAṄKARA

From Rājgira, he moved to Videha via many villages on the way. He reached Brāhmaṇ Kunda and stayed at a temple compound outside the town. A scholar, Ṛṣabhadatta, visited with his wife, Devānandā. According to *BS* 9.33.380, she was overwhelmed with motherly love as Mahāvīra was her biological son. They became his disciples, studied the eleven limbs of texts, and eventually attained liberation after many years of penance and meditation. In the west of Brāhmaṇkunda, Kṣatriyakunda's prince Jamāli also became his disciple with five hundred other Kṣatriyas. They also studied eleven limbs of texts and practised various kinds of penance and meditation. Jamāli's wife, Priyadarśanā, and one thousand other ladies followed suit (*BS* 9.33.384-6). In this way, Mahāvīra completed his fourteenth rainy season retreat at Vaiśālī.

THE THIRD YEAR AS THE TĪRTHAṄKARA

After Vaiśālī, he arrived at Kauśāmbī and stayed at the Chandrāvataraṇa temple compound. The local King Udayan, his mother Mṛgāvatī, and his paternal aunt Jayantī visited Mahāvīra and bowed to him. Jayantī asked profound spiritual questions to which Mahāvīra replied in detail:

Question: How is the soul light or heavy?

Answer: There are eighteen sins – violence, falsehood, stealing, sex, accumulation, anger, pride, illusion, greed, attachment, hatred, quarrel, accusing falsely, slandering, pleasures or displeasure from mundane things, criticism of other ideologies, deceit, and wrong ideologies, which cause the soul to be heavy and stuck in the transmigration cycle in four kinds of species – human, gods, demons, and *triyancha* (animals or plants). As the soul removes these *karma* particles, it becomes lighter, transcends the rebirth cycle, and attains liberation.

Question: Eligibility for liberation is by the soul's inherent nature or its efforts?

Answer: The soul is naturally capable of attaining liberation.

Question: Are all destined for liberation?

Answer: Yes, all are destined.

Question: In that case, will the world become empty of souls?

Answer: No. Just as the sky cannot be emptied by removing its particles one by one, the world cannot be emptied by the continuous liberation of souls because they are infinite. Later commentators added this explanation: although all seeds can ripen, not all seeds always ripen. Similarly, although clay is inherently capable of becoming a pot and a stone can become a statue, all clay or all stones can never become pots or statues.

Question: Is the soul better being awake or asleep?

Answer: Some souls are better awake and others asleep. Evil souls are better asleep when they cannot trouble the righteous ones. However, righteous souls are better awake as they are busy indulging in noble actions. Similarly, noble or evil usage of one's power, wealth, and means decides their nature.

Convinced by Mahāvīra's answers, Jayantī became his disciple (*BS* 12.2.443).

He then reached Śrāvastī from Kauśāmbī, where Sumanobhadra and Supratiṣṭha became his disciples. After many years of penance, both attained liberation at Vipulagiri in Rājgira. Then, Mahāvīra reached Vāṇiyagrām, where Ānand became a householder disciple. Mahāvīra completed his fifteenth rainy season retreat here.

THE FOURTH YEAR AS THE TĪRTHAṄKARA

After the rainy season, he headed towards Magadh. He reached Rājgira via different villages, where the son of a prominent wealthy man, Gobhadra and his son Śālibhadra renounced their luxuries and pleasures and became Mahāvīra's disciples. Śālibhadra's sister Subhadrā shared this news with her merchant husband Dhannā, who also immediately became Mahāvīra's disciple (*TSPC* 19.10.84 and 10.10.149-81). Thus, Mahāvīra continued his campaign to transform people spiritually and completed his sixteenth rainy season retreat at Rājgira.

THE FIFTH YEAR AS THE TĪRTHAṄKARA

Later, he arrived at Champā, where the local king visited him, and his son Mahāchandra became a disciple. After some time, when Mahāvīra revisited the town, the prince renounced his luxuries and five hundred women to become a monk (*VS* 2.9). After some time, in the scorching summer heat, Mahāvīra and his thousands of ascetic disciples started walking towards Vītabhayā town. As the congregation was suffering from heat, hunger and thirst, a group of carts carrying sesame appeared on the way. When the cart drivers offered sesame to the ascetics, Mahāvīra forbade them to keep their dietary discipline. At Vītabhayā, the local king Udrāyaṇ visited him, and many others became his disciples. His seventeenth rainy season retreat was at Vāṇiyagrām.

THE SIXTH YEAR AS THE TĪRTHAṄKARA

Afterwards, he arrived at Vārāṇasī, where the local king Jitaśatru visited him. Two prominent couples - Chullinī with his wife Śyāmā and Surādeva with his wife Dhānyā - became his householder disciples. From here, Mahāvīra reached Ālambhiyā, where a Hindu scholar, Pudgala, became his disciple (*BS* 2 11.12.436). Chulaśataka also became a householder disciple here. After visiting various other places, Mahāvīra reached Rājgira, where four more disciples joined as ascetics and a few more as householders. His eighteenth rainy season retreat was also here.

THE SEVENTH YEAR AS THE TĪRTHAṄKARA

Even after the rainy season, Mahāvīra continued staying at Rājgira. Once, in the presence of King Śreṇika, somebody blessed Mahāvīra to die soon and blessed Śreṇika to die late. Mahāvīra explained to Śreṇika that early death means early liberation, but late death would mean rebirth with suffering in hell (*AC* 169). To allay Śreṇika's concerns, Mahāvīra advised him that if a butcher can stop killing animals or a particular Brahmin woman can start donating, his suffering in hell can be avoided.

Śreṇika was further concerned when none of that happened. Mahāvīra then consoled him and predicted he would become a Tīrthaṅkara in one of his future lives. Later, Śreṇika announced that he would sponsor the family of anyone joining Mahāvīra's congregation, which inspired many people and thirteen queens to become Mahāvīra's disciples.

Mahāvīra spent his nineteenth rainy season retreat in Rājgira.

THE EIGHTH YEAR AS THE TĪRTHAṄKARA

From Rājgira, he reached Ālambhiyā and then Kauśāmbī. Here, Queen Mṛgāvatī was seeking a respite from Pradyota, who was desperate to marry her and surrounded the town with his army. After listening to Mahāvīra's renunciatory discourses, she was interested in joining his congregation, so she asked Pradyota, who was also in the assembly. Pradyota respectfully allowed her, and her dignity was not threatened (*AC* 1.91).

Later, Mahāvīra stayed in Vaiśālī for his twentieth rainy season retreat.

THE NINTH YEAR AS THE TĪRTHAṄKARA

After Vaiśālī, he moved to Kākandī via Mithilā and stayed at Sahasrāmra Garden. King Jitaśatru visited him and announced to sponsor anyone's family who joined the congregation. Dhanyakumāra, the son of a prominent wealthy family, was impressed and joined the congregation with permission from his mother. In Jitaśatru's presence, he renounced his luxurious life with thirty-two wives and studied the eleven limbs of texts after becoming a monk. He became one of the most ardent ascetics in his severe austere fasting practices among all the 14,000 monks. He left his body after being an ascetic for nine months. Sunakśatrakumāra also became a monk here and similarly left his body. From Kākandī, the congregation moved to Kampilpur, Polāspur and then Vāṇiyagrām. At Kampilpur, Kundakaulik became a householder disciple, and at Polāspur, Saddālputra accepted the twelve vows.

Later, Mahāvīra stayed in Vaiśālī for his twenty-first rainy season retreat.

THE TENTH YEAR AS THE TĪRTHAṄKARA

After Vaiśālī, he moved to Rājgira via Magadh. Here, Mahāśataka became his householder disciple, and Pārśvāpatya became a monk (*BS* 5.9). Another monk named Rohak asked some questions to which Mahāvīra responded as follows:

Question: What came first, *Loka* or *Aloka*?

Answer: There is no fixed sequence for either.

Question: What came first, *Jīva* or *Ajīva*?

Answer: Like *Loka* or *Aloka*, there is no fixed pattern for *Jīva* or *Ajīva* and for liberated or bonded souls.

Question: What came first, egg or chicken?

Answer: This is also a cycle without a clear beginning or end.

Continuing the questions, Gautama asked a few more:

Question: How is the earth upheld or supported? As some Hindu texts mention, is it on a serpent's head or a turtle's back?

Answer: The wind is on space, water is on the wind, the earth is on the water, the living beings are on the earth, the living beings support the nonliving things, depending on *karma*, the soul exists in different forms, the soul accumulates non-living pudgala particles of thoughts and speech, and *karma* accumulates in the soul.

He explained this with an example.

If a balloon is filled with air, and then after tying in the middle, if it is opened, all the air will be released from the upper half. Then, if it is filled with water, the upper half will contain water. Similarly, water is based on wind. As anybody with an inflated swimming ring would float in the water, a living being is sustained on the earth. Finally, as a boat with a few holes can have water inside and float on water, the soul and *karma* particles are bonded together. As the holes increase, the boat would sink. As *karma* particles increase, the soul sinks with less hope of crossing the rebirth cycle (*BS* 2.1.55).

With such discourses and discussions, he completed his twenty-second rainy season retreat at Rājgira.

THE ELEVENTH YEAR AS THE TĪRTHAṄKARA

Many Vedic scholars continued to join his congregation. After Rājgira, he came to Kṛtangalā-Kayangalā. In the nearby town of Śrāvastī lived a Vedic scholar named Skandak. While passing through his house, a non-Vedic scholar – named Pingal – asked, 'Is the universe finite or infinite? Are the souls, liberated beings, and liberation finite or infinite? What kind of death reduces or increases the soul's journey?' Unable to answer these questions, Skandak visited Mahāvīra just as Mahāvīra had predicted his joining the congregation. Mahāvīra's disciple, Gautama, asked Skandak about the questions raised by Pingal. Skandak gratefully and surprisingly shared the questions with Mahāvīra, who replied in detail:

Answer: There are four ways to describe the universe – by material, by space, by time, and by mode. The material universe is finite, the spatial universe is vast and finite, the temporal universe is both without a beginning and endless, and the soul's modes are infinite. Similar arguments apply to the souls, liberated beings, and liberation. Regarding death, it is of two types – childish and mature. The former death increases rebirth cycles, while the latter reduces it. Childish death is of twelve types, including ignorant death in anger, greed, or illusion (*BS* 2.1.91). Convinced by the answers, Skandak became a monk and left his body at Vipulāchal mountain after twelve years.

From Kayangalā, Mahāvīra went to Sāvatthī and then to Vāṇiyagrām.

He completed his twenty-third rainy season retreat at Vāṇiyagrām.

THE TWELFTH YEAR AS THE TĪRTHAṄKARA

After the rainy season, the congregation arrived at Brāhmaṇ-kunda, where Jamāli asked Mahāvīra to wander on a different route. Mahāvīra kept silent, so he took his five hundred disciples and proceeded separately. Mahāvīra's congregation reached Tungikā, via Rājgira, Kauśāmbī, and Vatsa. Mahāvīra agreed with Gautama's explanation of penance (*TSPC* 10.8.337-53) and added that ascetics benefit from listening to discourses, from listening to knowledge, from knowledge rationality, from rationality renunciation, from renunciation self-discipline, from discipline blockage of the influx of *karma*, from *karma* blockage penance, from penance destruction of *karma*, from *karma* destruction of non-action. Finally, non-action leads to liberation (*BS* 2 5.14.937). In the same year, Vehās, Abhay and other disciples successfully did penance at Vipulagiri and left their bodies there peacefully.

He completed his twenty-fourth rainy season retreat at Rājgira.

THE THIRTEENTH YEAR AS THE TĪRTHAṄKARA

After Rājgira, he reached Champā and gave discourses attended by the local ruler Kauṇik. Several householders were inspired and became ascetics, including the ten grandsons of Śreṇika. Jinapālit and others became ascetic disciples, and Pālit became a householder disciple.

The twenty-fifth rainy season retreat occurred at Champā.

THE FOURTEENTH YEAR AS THE TĪRTHAṄKARA

From Champā, he moved to Videha. On the way, at Kākandi, Khemak and Dhṛtidhar became ascetic disciples. Both performed penance for sixteen years at Vipulāchal and left their bodies peacefully. The ten local queens became disciples of Chandanā (Mahāvīra's first female ascetic disciple, as mentioned earlier) and left their bodies after penance.

The twenty-sixth rainy season retreat occurred at Mithila.

THE FIFTEENTH YEAR AS THE TĪRTHAṄKARA

After the rainy season, the congregation moved towards Śrāvastī. Kauṇik's brothers Halla and Vehalla, who caused the war in Vaiśālī, visited Mahāvīra and became his ascetic disciples.

Encounter with Makkhali Gośāla and His Death

Makkhali Gośāla, who had separated from Mahāvīra in his tenth year of penance, spent most of his time around Śrāvastī. He founded the ideology *Ājīvika* and proclaimed himself to be a Tīrthaṅkara. Mahāvīra's disciple Gautama heard about this from other Tīrthaṅkara, but Mahāvīra explained in detail who Makkhali Gośāla was. Gośāla was outside the town and heard about this conversation. He rushed to stay at a potter's place, one of his two disciples in the town. He spoke with his congregation in anger and jealousy. Mahāvīra's disciple Ānand was wandering there for alms. Gośāla warned him that he would destroy Mahāvīra if he tried to slander him. Frightened Ānand, shared the conversation with Mahāvīra. Mahāvīra assured him that no one could destroy a Tīrthaṅkara and told all his disciples to ignore Gośāla, who was advancing towards their congregation.

As soon as Ānand announced Mahāvīra's message to the entire congregation, Gośāla arrived there. He told Mahāvīra that the earlier Gośāla, who used to be his disciple, died long ago, and now he is in his seventh subsequent lifespan but in the same body as the earlier Gośāla. However, Mahāvīra rejected his claim and compared him with a thief trying to hide his identity behind a grass stick. At that Gośāla furiously started abusing and cursing Mahāvīra. Mahāvīra and all his disciples remained calm, but one monk, Sarvānubhuti, tried to respond but was immediately killed by Gośāla. As Gośāla continued abusing Mahāvīra, another monk from Ayodhyā, Sunakṣatra, tried to stop him but was also fiercely attacked by Gośāla. Sunakṣatra apologised to Mahāvīra and his congregation and passed On. Mahāvīra tried to stop Gośāla, but Gośāla tried killing Mahāvīra. However, the attack backfired, leaving Mahāvīra untouched, but Gośāla severely battered. Gośāla cursed Mahāvīra to die within six months. However, Mahāvīra prophesied that he would leave his body after sixteen years, but Gośāla would die within seven days. With directions from Mahāvīra, his disciples overpowered Gośāla in debates, but he could not respond due to his severe rage. This conflict became the talk of the town, and more people started accepting Mahāvīra as the true Tīrthaṅkara (*BS* 2 15.553.678).

Mahāvīra told his congregation that Gośāla's destructive power used against him was sufficient to destroy sixteen kingdoms. Meanwhile, injured Gośāla returned to the potter's place with his congregation. To soothe his injuries and suffering, he tried raw mangoes, alcohol, and cool water from clay pots. He foresaw his imminent death and told his disciples to bathe his dead body in scented water, dry it up with a scented towel, apply sandalwood paste, cover in valuable white clothes, decorate with expensive jewellery, and declare that the twenty-fourth Tīrthaṅkara attained liberation (*BS* 2 15.553.678). However, Gośāla's illusion disappeared by the seventh night, and he regretted his actions. He told his disciples again that the true Tīrthaṅkara is Mahāvīra. He told them to spit thrice on his dead body and pull it across the town, exposing his falsehood. On the seventh night, he passed away. Instead of disparaging him publicly, his disciples took out a small procession within the potter's house following his instruction. Then, they had the actual procession across the town and cremated him.

Interestingly, before attaining omniscience, Mahāvīra protected Gośāla from attacks. However, after becoming Tīrthaṅkara, Mahāvīra did not protect his disciples from Gośāla's lethal attacks. Before omniscience, Mahāvīra had not fully transcended attachments and aversions and protected his disciple Gośāla. However, becoming omniscient, Mahāvīra could foresee the fate of his disciples, so he did not interfere in their predestined deaths as he was beyond all attachments or aversions (*AS* 1.9.4.15).

From Śrāvastī, he started for Janapada and reached Medhiyāgrām. Here, he suffered from bleeding diarrhoea and the past lethal attacks from Gośāla but bore the suffering calmly. People worried he might die in six months due to these health issues. Mahāvīra sent for one such monk, Sīhā, who cried with concern for Mahāvīra's health. Mahāvīra assured him that he would live for sixteen more years and told him to visit the house of Revatī, a local household, who prepared the medicine for his treatment. However, Sīhā asked Revatī for the leftover dish made from Citron fruit,[1] not the medicine. Pleasantly surprised to note that Mahāvīra knew about her kitchen items, she happily donated the dish, which cured Mahāvīra's suffering (*BS* 2 15.1.557).

Next, Mahāvīra reached Mithilā and completed the seventh rainy season retreat. In the same year, Jamali developed differences with Mahāvīra and left the congregation, while Sudarśanā joined it. In answering Gautama's questions, Mahāvīra mentioned that Gośāla and the two monks killed by Gośāla would all attain increasingly better rebirths and would attain liberation eventually (*BS* 2 15.1.560-95).

THE SIXTEENTH YEAR AS THE TĪRTHAṄKARA

From Mithilā, he moved to Hastināpur. Meanwhile, Gautama and his disciples reached Śrāvastī, where Keśi from the lineage of the twenty-third Tīrthaṅkara Pārśva was staying in a nearby park. Ascetics in both congregations, being in the same town, developed doubts based on their differences. Monks following Parsavaid not practice nudity, unlike Mahāvīra's monks. Pārśva's lineage practices were based on only four major vows, unlike the five major vows of Mahāvīra's congregation. Realizing these issues, Gautama visited Keśi, and both sat together with their congregations and other visitors. Keśi asked twelve questions, to which Gautama responded.

Question: Pārśva preached four vows, whereas Mahāvīra five. What is the reason for adding the fifth vow?

Answer: Dharma is taught according to people's capacity to comprehend and practice. During the first Tīrthaṅkara Ṛṣabha, people were unpretentious, making it difficult to make them understand. Contrariwise, during the current twenty-fourth Tīrthaṅkara Mahāvīra, people are crooked, making it difficult to make them practice. Therefore, the first and twenty-fourth Tīrthaṅkaras preached five major vows. However, the followers of the second to twenty-third Tīrthaṅkaras were more ingenuous and intellectually more profound and understood and practised the succinct Dharmic message correctly. The number of vows in different eras reflected the precision of understanding and ease of practice.

Question: Why did Pārśva not require nudity, whereas Mahāvīra did?

Answer: External appearance and behaviour are based on social customs and contemporary practice. However, the ultimate emphasis is only on the right knowledge, faith, and conduct, and external practices such as clothes become irrelevant.

Question: If thousands of enemies are invading you, how will you defeat them?

Answer: By conquering one, five are conquered. By conquering five, ten are conquered. By conquering the ten, all the enemies are conquered. An unrestrained mind is our enemy, as are five sense organs and four kinds of attachments and aversions. Mind control allows one to control the sense organs and live freely and triumphantly.

Question: Many worldly creatures are seen bonded, but how do you live freely?

Answer: I live freely by severing the bonds of attachments and aversions.

Question: How have you severed the vine growing inside the heart and producing toxic fruits?

Answer: I have completely uprooted the vine of desires and live freely.

Question: How have you extinguished the intense and potentially deadly fire inside the body?

Answer: I douse the fire with the water of knowledge from Mahāvīra. In the spiritual realm, passions are fire, while exemplary character and penance are water that protects us from the fire of passion or aversion.

Question: Why do you ride but not fall off a courageous, cruel horse running fast?

Answer: The horse, i.e. the mind, takes me to spiritually progressive goals as I appropriately restrain it with spiritual knowledge from Mahāvīra.

Question: Unlike many lost travellers, how do you not wander away from your path?

Answer: I know both paths, spiritually progressive and regressive. The only path that Tīrthaṅkara leads is to be followed, and the rest must be avoided.

Question: Worldly creatures are blown away by the storms of the world. Who do you consider the island of sanctuary in such a scenario?

Answer: In the flow of old age and death in the world, Dharma protects like a large island in the world's ocean as the ultimate sanctuary.

Question: How will you ride a boat and cross an ocean with an intense flow?

Answer: A boat can be of two types – with holes that cannot float or without holes that can. The body is the boat, and the soul is the sailor of this boat. A body without the influx of *karma* enables sages to cross the worldly ocean.

Question: Who can enlighten the worldly creatures wandering in the dark?

Answer: The sun has already arisen to enlighten the world. The omniscient Tīrthaṅkara is the sun that can enlighten the darkened world.

Question: What can be the peaceful refuge for worldly creatures suffering from physical and mental pains?

Answer: At the final frontier of the universe, there is a fixed place devoid of death, old age, disease, and suffering. However, it is not readily available for all. It is called Nirvāṇa, Kṣema, Siddhi, or Śivasthāna. Ascetics reaching this destination are free from all sufferings.

Keśi joined Mahāvīra's congregation after listening to Gautama's answers. Meanwhile, Mahāvīra reached Hastināpura, where the local king Śiva joined his congregation, studied the eleven limbs of the texts, and left the body after intense penance (*BS* 2 11.9.418). Pottilla and many others followed suit.

Later, Mahāvīra reached Vāṇiyagrām, where he completed his twenty-eighth rainy season retreat.

THE SEVENTEENTH YEAR AS THE TĪRTHAṄKARA

After the rainy season, Mahāvīra left Videha and came to Rājgira via Magadh. Besides Mahāvīra's followers, Rājgira had other groups, including Buddhists and *Ājivikas*. Once Mahāvīra explained to Gautama about the *Ājivikas*, whose many practices are like his congregation. They revere the Arihantas and respect their parents. They avoid five fruits – fig, plum, mulberry, banyan, peepal (sacred fig), and root vegetables such as onion and garlic. They avoid causing injuries to bulls. Many ascetics left their bodies that year at Vipulāchal at Rājgira, where the congregation completed the twenty-ninth rainy season retreat.

THE EIGHTEENTH YEAR AS THE TĪRTHAṄKARA

After the rainy season, the congregation moved to Champā and stayed in the town's western part. The local king Śāla and his younger brother Mahāśāla became monks after listening to Mahāvīra's discourses. King's maternal nephew, Gāngalī, was appointed the new king. Then, Mahāvīra moved to the central part of the town, where a householder, Kāmadeva, came to listen to him having delegated business to his son. Mahāvīra asked him about his last night when he avoided the temptations. Upon confirmation, Mahāvīra shared Kāmadeva's superior moral strength with his ascetics (*UDS* 2.114). Then, the congregation moved to Daśārṇapur, where the local king, Daśārṇabhadra, realised his false pride, renounced all his wealth, and became a monk. Later, the congregation reached Vāṇiyagrām, where Somil, a prominent Vedic scholar, visited Mahāvīra with his one hundred students and asked several complex questions before accepting his discipleship:

Question: What is the ideal kind of journey?

Answer: The real journey is to be aware and indulge in penance, vows, restraint, self-study, meditation, and other required spiritual practices (*BS* 18.10.646).

Question: What is Yāpanīya[2]?

Answer: Yāpanīya is of two kinds, with or without sense organs. I practice the former by restraining my listening, seeing, smelling, tasting, and touching. I practice the latter by preventing and controlling anger, pride, illusion, and greed.

Question: What is Avyābādha?

Answer: Avyābādha is preventing and controlling diseases arising from the imbalance of *Vāta* (wind), *Pitta* (bile) and *Kapha* (phlegm).

Question: What is Prāsuka Vihāra?

Answer: Carefully walking and resting by avoiding inappropriate locations is Prāsuka Vihāra.

Question. Is Sarisava edible or not?

Answer: Sarisava can be edible and inedible, depending on its two meanings. The former ones with similar timespan are inedible for my ascetics. The latter is mustard, which can be of two kinds. Only naturally fallen seeds are edible, and that too if they are asked for and received in alms; otherwise, they are inedible. Therefore, they can be both edible and inedible.

Question: Is Māsa edible or not?

Answer: Māsa can be edible and inedible, depending on the context. One temporal meaning of the word is month, which is inedible. The material meaning of the word is of two types: economic, which is inedible, and pulse, which is edible. My ascetics can consume the pulses if they are accepted in alms. Any raw pulse or seed is also inedible because it has consciousness.

Question: Is Kulatthā edible or not?

Answer: Kulatthā can also be edible and inedible. Its first meaning is a cultured lady, which is not for consumption. The second meaning refers to pulses, which are edible if they are unconscious (cooked) and are accepted in alms.

After the satisfactory answers to his strange questions above, he tried testing Mahāvīra's philosophical knowledge with the following questions:

Question: Are you one or two? Are you eternal and imperishable, or do you have multiple modes temporarily?

Answer: I am both one and two. I am eternal and imperishable. I also have multiple modes at various times and in various contexts. In substance, I am the soul. Since the soul never perishes, I am eternal and imperishable. However, the soul takes different bodies at various times, so I also change my modes.

Based on Anekāntavāda, Mahāvīra answered his several mystifying questions on duality, nonduality, and many other philosophical topics. Impressed with the detailed elucidations, Somil became his householder disciple and left his body after intense penance.

The congregation completed the thirtieth rainy season retreat at Vāṇiyagrām.

THE NINETEENTH YEAR AS THE TĪRTHAṄKARA

After the rainy season, Mahāvīra's congregation moved towards Pānchāl via Sāket and Sāvatthi and reached outside Kampilpur. Here, a Brahmin Ambad lived with his seven hundred disciples and, after listening to Mahāvīra, became his householder disciple with his other disciples. He practised strict discipline matching many rules of Mahāvīra's congregation, such as celibacy, containment, non-accumulation of things, non-violence, and truthfulness. He avoided harming even water, so he did not enter any river, well, or pond. He did not ride any vehicle, such as a chariot, and did not ride on any animal, such as an elephant or horse. Like Mahāvīra's congregation, he only walked. He avoided watching plays, shows, and dramas and telling stories. He did not even touch green vegetables or plants. He collected alms only in clay or wooden pots, avoiding gold, silver, or copper utensils. He wore only an ochre sheet, avoiding other colours. He wore only a copper garland and an ear ornament, avoiding other jewellery and flower garland. He avoided applying saffron or sandalwood paste on his body and applied only soil from the Ganga basin. He did not accept specially cooked food for himself or the food bought or brought by somebody else. He used little water for drinking and bathing, which must also be filtered and collected in alms. He did not fetch water from a water body. He fasted for a month and left his body peacefully. His disciples also fasted and passed away in a forest where they could not find a donor to provide water to them.

From Kampilpur, Mahāvīra's congregation moved to Vaiśālī.

Their thirty-first rainy season retreat occurred here.

THE TWENTIETH YEAR AS THE TĪRTHAṄKARA

After the rainy season, the congregation once again reached Vāṇiyagrām. During one of Mahāvīra's discourses, an ascetic from Pārśva's lineage, Gāngeya, visited and asked if the Hellish beings were born continuously or continually. In his usual Anekāntavāda way, Mahāvīra replied that they could be born either way. Convinced by answers to many such questions, he became a monk in the congregation (*BS* 9.5). After wandering through nearby places, the congregation spent its second rainy season at Vaiśālī.

THE TWENTY-FIRST YEAR AS THE TĪRTHAṄKARA

After the rainy season, the congregation moved to Magadh and Rājgira. Ascetics from many other sects stayed nearby, and vigorous debates occurred among them about their ideologies. Gautama developed some doubts, having heard other viewpoints, which Mahāvīra clarified. He specifically mentioned that the soul and *jīva* are the same. Once, Madduka, a faithful householder disciple of Mahāvīra, was challenged by folks from other groups:

Question: How could you believe the words of his guru without seeing the reality?

Answer: The wind flows, but can you see its colour? Can you see the particles of a fragrance? You also believe in your ancient lineage, ancestors, heavens, and the final boundary of the universe without seeing them.

Later, Mahāvīra praised his responses, which left the sceptics speechless. When Gautama asked if Madduka would become a monk, Mahāvīra replied negatively but confirmed that Madduka would spiritually progress as a householder and, in a future life, would attain liberation.

After wandering nearby places, the congregation spent its thirty-third rainy season at Rājgira.

THE TWENTY-SECOND YEAR AS THE TĪRTHAṄKARA

After visiting various places in the early winter, they returned to Rājgira. Once, Gautama was returning after alms collection and was stopped by the same people who questioned Madduka earlier, as mentioned earlier. Unsatisfied with Gautama's response, they visited Mahāvīra, who asked them if they wanted to discuss the five *dravyas* (substances) – *jīva* (soul), *pudgala* (matter), *dharma* (medium of motion), *adharma* (medium of rest), and *ākāśa* (space). Mahāvīra told them that only *pudgala* could enable physical actions, such as walking, sleeping, or sitting. However, *karma* happened only to the soul, not to the *pudgala*. Convinced by the detailed explanations, they requested a discourse also. After listening, they joined the congregation as ascetics and became good scholars after studying the eleven limbs of the texts (*BS* 7.10.305).

The congregation moved to Nālandā, a suburb located in Rājgira's north-east. Udak Pedhāla, an ascetic of the Pārśva lineage, visited Gautama and asked about a vow that a householder joining the congregation takes – not to cause any violence to any living mobile being (trasa) except to help catch a criminal as ordered by the local authorities. However, this vow has an implicit moral issue because immobile beings (*sthāvara*) can be reborn as mobile beings (trasa) and vice versa. Therefore, the mobile beings that were not to be harmed change to immobile beings that are allowed to be harmed. The vow should mention mobile and past-mobile beings also. Gautama rejected this advice by stating that a householder's focus is the present life of a being, not the past or future lives. Those who cannot renounce violence with the ascetic vow can only take the householder vow and limit their violence to the best extent possible. There is no need to rectify this vow (*SK* 2.7.72-4). Senior monks also came along, so Gautama asked them a similar question. A householder who vows not to hurt any ascetic kills a householder who used to be an ascetic earlier. Will this crime accrue the same sin as killing an ascetic? The senior monks answered negatively. Gautama concluded that the past modes of any being were irrelevant in maintaining the vows. Udak, inspired by detailed explanations, joined Mahāvīra's congregation as a monk (*SK* 2.7.81).

After wandering in nearby towns, the congregation spent its thirty-fourth rainy season at Nālandā.

THE TWENTY-THIRD YEAR AS THE TĪRTHAṄKARA

After the rainy season, they reached Videha's capital, Vāṇijyagrām,[3] an important trading centre. Among thousands of people attending Mahāvīra's discourses, Sudarśana, a prominent business leader, also joined and asked some questions after the crowd left. Mahāvīra explained various kinds of time and the infinite time cycle, *Palyopama*. Mahāvīra also told him about his past life, which overwhelmed him, and he renounced the world became an ascetic instantly. He studied eleven limbs of the texts, and after twelve years of penance, he passed away peacefully (*BS* 11.11.424-32).

Once, Gautama was returning after alms collection and met Ānand, Mahāvīra's householder disciple, who was fasting. Frail Ānand could not get up, but as Gautama approached him, he bowed to him and shared his newly attained mystical power. Intrigued, Gautama asked Mahāvīra if a householder could receive such power. After Mahāvīra affirmed, Gautama returned to Ānand and admitted and apologised for his earlier scepticism.

After wandering in nearby towns, the congregation spent its thirty-fifth rainy season retreat at Vaiśālī.

THE TWENTY-FOURTH YEAR AS THE TĪRTHAṄKARA

After the rainy season, the congregation wandered in the Kauśala region and arrived at Sāketa, a famous town. Amidst a large crowd attending Mahāvīra's preaching assembly, Jinadeva, a jeweller and a king visiting from another kingdom, also visited the assembly. The king bowed to Mahāvīra and asked about the jewels. Mahāvīra explained that jewels are of two types – physical and spiritual. Spiritual jewels, in turn, are of three types: faith, knowledge and conduct. The three jewels of the latter types are so influential that they enhance the one who owns and practices them. They also ensure a better life in the present and future. While physical jewels are limited in providing pleasure only in the current life, spiritual jewels provide bliss beyond the current life. The wisdom inspired the visiting king, who became a monk in the congregation (*ĀN* 1305).

Then, the congregation moved to Kampilpur, Sūrsen, Mathurā, Sauripur, and Nandīpur and finally returned to Mithilā, where the thirty-sixth rainy season retreat occurred.

THE TWENTY-FIFTH YEAR AS THE TĪRTHAṄKARA

After the rainy season, the congregation reached Rājgira via many villages where Mahāvīra preached. Once, ascetic Kālodāyī asked Mahāvīra how one indulges in *karma* with evil consequences. Mahāvīra explained that it is like consuming intoxicating or unhealthy food to gratify the taste buds for some time. Lost in the short-term taste, one forgets the impending harm, leading to detrimental aftermaths on one's body. In the same way, when one is involved in violence, falsehood, theft, sexual misconduct, possession of materials, anger, pride, illusion, greed and attachment or aversion, they all appear pleasing and alluring. However, they all result in unfavourable consequences for the perpetrators. He then asked how one indulges in auspicious *karma*. Mahāvīra elucidated that one is forced to eat medicinal food even though it tastes bitter and intense. Its nutritional values provide health benefits. Similarly, practising non-violence, truth, noble conduct, forgiveness and altruism appears difficult prima facie. They are often performed half-heartedly but bring long-term advantages (*BS* 2 7.10.306).

He then asked about two people, one of whom started the fire while the other extinguished. Mahāvīra clarified that the one who started the fire caused more violence to the earth, water, wind and other beings, while the one who dowsed the fire reduced the violence to the earth, water, wind and other beings. Therefore, the latter's *karma* consequences will be less than the former's (*BS* 7.10.307). Then, he asked about non-conscious *pudgala*, to which Mahāvīra replied that its usage causes violence and the user becomes violent. *Pudgalas* are non-conscious as jewels too are.

Convinced with the answers, Kālodāyī bowed to Mahāvīra, continued fasts for six and eight days, and eventually left his body. In the same year, Prabhāsa, one of the eleven chief disciples, Gaṇadharas, passed away.

The thirty-seventh rainy season retreat occurred at Rājgira.

THE TWENTY-SIXTH YEAR AS THE TĪRTHAṄKARA

After the rainy season, the congregation arrived at Nālandā, where Gautama asked Mahāvīra about particles' fission and fusion, linguistics, and the artificiality of sorrow. Achalabhrātā and Metārya, two more of the eleven chief disciples, passed away that year after fasting.

The thirty-eighth rainy season retreat occurred at Nālandā.

THE TWENTY-SEVENTH YEAR AS THE TĪRTHAṄKARA

Afterwards, they moved to Mithilā in the Videha region, where the local king, Jitaśatru, came and bowed to Mahāvīra. After the audience left the preaching assembly, Gautama asked Mahāvīra about the sun and its movement, the moon and its movement, light and shadow, the beginning of the year, moon phases, planetary motion, and the distance between the moon and sun.

The thirty-ninth rainy season retreat occurred at Mithilā.

THE TWENTY-EIGHTH YEAR AS THE TĪRTHAṄKARA

After wandering in nearby towns, the congregation spent its fortieth rainy season retreat at Mithilā. Many more became disciples as ascetics or householders.

THE TWENTY-NINTH YEAR AS THE TĪRTHAṄKARA

After the rainy season, the congregation moved to Magadh and returned to Rājgira, where a householder, Mahāśataka, was doing his ultimate penance. Annoyed by one of his wives, Revati's frequent mischiefs, he cursed her to die and be reborn in hell within a week. Afterwards, Mahāvīra sent Gautama to ask Mahāśataka to repent his action (*UDS* 8.257-61). Later, Mahāvīra explained about a hot waterfall in which living and nonliving beings of warm nature keep flowing into it (*BS* 2.5.113). Responding to another question on happiness and sadness, he gave an example of particles of a fragrant gas that can be spread across a vast area but cannot be collected back (*BS* 6.9.253). Similarly, happiness and sadness cannot be accumulated in any manner.

After fasting, two more of the eleven chief disciples, Agnibhūti and Vāyubhūti, passed away that year.

The congregation spent its forty-first rainy season retreat at Rājgira.

THE THIRTIETH YEAR AS THE TĪRTHAṄKARA

After fasting for one month, three more of the eleven chief disciples, Avyakta, Mandita and Akampita, passed away during this period. Once, Gautama asked Mahāvīra about the situation in the most negative period, the sixth era of the present time cycle. His last rainy season retreat was at Pāvāpurī, where he preached about the sanctity and dignity of every creature. Death, sorrow and offence are unacceptable to each. Therefore, all beings should avoid behaviour that is unpleasant to them. All should behave with others just as they expect others to behave with them – the foundational principle of humanity and dharma, practising which one attains ultimate liberation. Otherwise, one wanders in the rebirth cycle. After the discourse, the local king Puṇyapāla bowed to him and shared his concerns about the eight dreams from last night in which he saw an elephant, a monkey, a wild plant, a crow, a feeble lion, lotus, seed, and a waterpot. Mahāvīra interpreted the dreams in the following manner:

Elephant: In the future, even sensible householders will live like a furious elephant. Even in extreme or vulnerable situations, they would never consider renunciation. A rare few who choose asceticism would succumb to temptations and either abandon their path or fulfil their vows incorrectly, and even fewer would strongly follow their monastic vows.

Monkey: The monkey symbolises that in the future, even the senior ascetics who would lead the large congregations would exhibit the erratic nature of a monkey. They would be a little courageous and indolent in practising their vows. The corrupt people would ridicule even the genuine monastics who flawlessly follow their ascetic rules and preach the authentic dharma. The crooked people would severely disparage the sacred texts. This way, most people would be irrational and unstable like a monkey.

Wild plant: In the future, charlatan renunciants would surround even those householders donating little. Such donors would regard jackal-like lethargic ascetics as disciplined. The earth would be filled with fraudsters like thorny wild plants everywhere.

Crow: Like crows, most ascetics would noisily argue against authentic preachers. They would defy their self-discipline and join sham sects.

Feeble Lion: The lion-like firm and radiant Jainism would become timid. Instead, various jackal-like phoney dharmas would be practised and respected more widely.

Lotus: Like a lotus in the mud, even noble people would fall into evil company and get misguided.

Seed: An ignorant farmer sows even a good seed in an infertile land and a bad seed in a fertile land. Similarly, in the future, householders would abandon the worthwhile ascetics and support the fake ones.

Waterpot: The last dream signifies that the ascetics with great qualities such as penance, renunciation and forgiveness would be rare to find in the future. Most of the corrupt ones would detest and quarrel with the noble ones. However, the householders would not be able to distinguish the two kinds of ascetics and would similarly treat them.

After having listened to these elucidations, the king was filled with renunciation from worldly life and became an ascetic. Eventually, after performing many austere practices, he left his body. In the fourth month of his last rainy season retreat, he gave his last discourse attended by rulers of several republics.

NOTES

1. Some European scholars in early twentieth century interpreted this to meat but admitted their mistake after objections and

clarifiations from the contemporary Jain community (Hastīmal 1971: 647-8).

2. Yāpanīya was also the name of a Jain sect that later merged with the other two major sects Digambara and Śvētāmbara (Dundas 2002: 48).
3. Vāṇijyagrām and Vāṇiyagrām are synonymously mentioned.

CHAPTER 4

Parinirvāṇa
Liberation

Mahāvīra spent thirty years as a householder, twelve years as a wandering renunciate and about thirty years as an omniscient preacher, i.e. Tīrthaṅkara. All Jain texts mention his lifespan to be seventy-two years. He spent his first rainy season retreat at Asthigrām, twelve retreats at Vaiśālī and Vāṇijyagrām, fourteen retreats at Rājgīr and Nālandā, six at Mithilā, two at Bhaddiyā Nagarī, one each at Ālambhikā and Sāvatthī, one at Vajrabhūmi, and one final at Pāvāpurī.

According to the Hindu calendar, Mahāvīra left his body on the new moon night of the Kartik month, now widely celebrated as Diwālī by Hindus and Jains worldwide. His final discourse covered fifty-five topics of good deeds, fifty-five topics of bad deeds, and thirty-six other topics later compiled in *Uttarādhyayana Sūtra*. According to the Jain texts, Mahāvīra attained liberation at Pāvāpurī near Rājgira, a town in the Patna district in the current Bihar state of India.[1] Just before his Nirvāṇa, he sent his foremost disciple, Indrabhuti Gautam, to meet a Brahmin named Devasharmā. Gautam also transcended his attachment to his guru and attained Nirvāṇa as soon as he got the news. Mahāvīra's body was cremated in the presence of eighteen local heads of the republics, who started the tradition of celebrating the life and message of Mahāvīra by lighting lamps across their regions that later became the festival of Diwālī, as mentioned. During his time, his seven hundred monks and 1,400 nuns also attained Nirvāṇa. In addition to 14,000 monks and 36,000 nuns, he had 1,59,000 laymen and 3,18,000 laywomen disciples.

MAHĀVĪRA'S CHIEF MALE DISCIPLES

He had nine groups in his congregations with eleven heads of these groups – Indrabhūti, Agnibhūti, Vayubhūti, Vyakta, Sudharmā, Mandita, Mauryaputra, Akampita, Achalabhrātā, Metārya and Prabhāsa – who were all Brahmins from various regions and had visited Pāvāpurī to attend a religious ceremony hosted by a Saumil Brahmin. They visited Mahāvīra with their disciples and joined his congregation on the same day as their questions were convincingly answered by Mahāvīra one by one.

1. Indrabhūti – He was the son of a Gautama Brahmin of the Gobara village in the Magadh kingdom. His parents were Vasubhūti and Pṛthvī. A scholar of the Vedas and Vedanta, he and his five hundred students became Mahāvīra's disciples after his query about Mahāvīra's discourse resolved his query about the soul. He was fifty at that time and spent thirty years in penance. He attained omniscience after Mahāvīra's death and spent twelve years as an omniscient. He left his body at ninety-two after a month-long fast. He was known for his humility, healthy body, and strict penance.
2. Agnibhūti – He was a younger brother of Indrabhūti. At forty-six, he and his five hundred students joined Mahāvīra's congregation after Mahāvīra's discourse resolved his query about non-dualism. He spent twelve years in penance and

sixteen years as an omniscient. At the age of seventy-four, he left his body in Mahāvīra's presence.

3. Vayubhūti – He was also a younger brother of Indrabhūti and Agnibhūti. Like his older brothers, he and his five hundred students also became Mahāvīra's disciples after listening to Mahāvīra's discourse on the souls. At forty-two, he began his journey as a wandering monk for the next ten years. After attaining omniscience, he lived for the next eighteen years. Two months before Mahāvīra's death, he left his body after a month-long fast at the age of seventy years.
4. Vyakta – He was a Bhārdwāja Brahmin from Kollāga. His parents were Dhanamitra and Vāruṇī. Like others, he and his five hundred students joined Mahāvīra's congregation after Mahāvīra's discourse resolved his query about the reality of the world other than Brahma. He was initiated at the age of fifty years, spent twelve years in penance, eighteen years as omniscient, and passed away at the age of eighty years after a month-long fast in Mahāvīra's presence.
5. Sudharmā – The fifth chief was a Vaiśyāyana Brahmin from Kollāga. His parents were Dhammila and Bhaddilā. He and his five hundred students also joined Mahāvīra's congregation as their doubts about rebirth were resolved by Mahāvīra's discourse. He led the congregation for twenty years after Mahāvīra's passing away. He spent fifty years as a householder, forty-two years in penance, seven years as an omniscient, and passed away at the age of one hundred.
6. Mandita – He was a Vasiṣṭha Brahmin from the Maurya region. His parents were Dhanadeva and Vijayādevī. With his three hundred and fifty students, he also joined Mahāvīra's congregation after his doubts about the soul were resolved by Mahāvīra's discourse. He started his

ascetic journey at the age of fifty-three, became omniscient at sixty-seven, and passed away at eighty three in Mahāvīra's presence.

7. Mauryaputra – He was a Kāśyapa Brahmin from the Maurya region. His parents were Maurya and Vijayādevī. At the age of sixty-five, he and his three hundred and fifty students joined Mahāvīra's congregation after his doubts about the heavens and heavenly gods and goddesses were resolved by Mahāvīra's discourse. He spent fourteen years in penance, became omniscient at seventy-nine, and passed away at ninty-five in Mahāvīra's presence.
8. Akampita – He was a Gautama Brahmin from the Mithilā region. His parents were Deva and Jayantī. At the age of forty-eight, he and his three hundred students joined Mahāvīra's congregation after his doubts about the hells and hellish beings were resolved by Mahāvīra's discourse. He spent nine years in penance, became omniscient at fifty-seven, and passed away at seventy-eight in Mahāvīra's last year.
9. Achalabhrātā – He was a Hārīta Brahmin from the Kauśalā region. His parents were Vasu and Nandā. At forty six, he and his three hundred students joined Mahāvīra's congregation after his doubts about spiritual merits and sins were resolved by Mahāvīra's discourse. He spent twelve years in penance, became omniscient at fifty-eight, and passed away at seventy-two after a month-long fast.
10. Metārya – He was a Kaudinya Brahmin from the Tungika region. His parents were Datta and Varuṇā. At the age of thirty-six years, he and his three hundred students joined Mahāvīra's congregation after his doubts about rebirth were resolved by Mahāvīra's discourse. He spent ten years in penance, became omniscient at forty-six, and passed away at sixty two in Mahāvīra's presence.

11. Prabhāsa – He was a Kaudinya Brahmin from the Rājgīra region. His parents were Bala and Atibhadrā. At the age of sixteen, he and his three hundred students joined Mahāvīra's congregation after his doubts about liberation were resolved by Mahāvīra's discourse. He spent eight years in penance, became omniscient at twenty-four, and passed away at forty after a month-long fast in Mahāvīra's presence.

MAHĀVĪRA'S FIRST FEMALE DISCIPLE

Princess Chandanā or Chandanabālā became Mahāvīra's first female disciple. Her parents were King Dadhivāhana and Queen Dhāriṇī, who named their daughter Vasumatī. The king escaped when their kingdom was invaded, but the queen committed suicide after the soldiers captured her. A wealthy merchant purchased the adolescent princess from the soldiers trying to trade her as an enslaved person. The merchant's family named her Chandanā. As her beauty and youth blossomed, the merchant's envious wife, as soon as the merchant away, turned against her by cutting her lengthy hair, chaining her limbs, and imprisoning her after beating her mercilessly. As mentioned earlier, Chandanā stayed incarcerated in the basement for three days without food or water. After the merchant returned home, he freed her, fed her some lentil seeds and rushed to fetch an ironsmith to cut her shackles. As she came outside to look for a guest to feed before ingesting lentil seeds Mahāvīra walked by, so she tried to offer him the same. When he refused to accept the seeds, tears rolled from her eyes. Seeing her tears, he accepted the seeds as all the conditions for his vow were fulfilled.

As the news of this significant donation spread widely, the king and queen visited her and took her back to the palace. As

Mahāvīra attained omniscience, she became the first nun in his congregation, led the nun's order, continued her penance, and attained Nirvāṇa.

HISTORICAL ANALYSIS OF MAHĀVĪRA'S NIRVĀṆA

Based on several Jain texts, scholars widely accept 527 BCE as Mahāvīra's Nirvāṇa year. German scholar Hermann Jacobi discussed Buddha's and Mahāvīra's Nirvāṇa in two different contexts, in a contradictary way. At one place, he mentioned 526 BCE as Mahāvīra's Nirvāṇa year, and elsewhere, he mentioned 477 BCE as that year. On the day of Mahāvīra's Nirvāṇa, King Pālak was coronated in Ujjain, who ruled for sixty years. Then, the Nandas ruled for hundred and fifty-five years, and afterwards, Maurya rule started. Therefore, Chandragupta was coronated two hundred and fifteen years after Mahāvīra's Nirvāṇa year, as is widely accepted among scholars today. Unfortunately, Jakobi neglected to add the sixty years of Pālak and took only hundred and fifty-five years of the Nandas, leading to the faulty calculation. Similarly, Jain monk Hemachandra mentioned that sixteen hundred sixty nine years after Mahāvīra's Nirvāṇa year, King Kumārpāl would be coronated, which is widely accepted to be CE 1143. Therefore, according to Hemachandra's calculation (1669–1142), Mahāvīra's Nirvāṇa proves to be CE 527, discrediting Jakobi's dates.

According to eminent historian K.P. Jayaswal,[2] Mahāvīra attained his liberation in 546 BCE, two years before the Buddha did in 544 BCE, citing the southern traditions of Buddhism. Other eminent historians, Radha Kumud Mukherjee and Jin Vijay have established that the Buddha left his body after Mahāvīra did. According to prominent Buddhist scholar Dharmananda Kosambi, among the seven contemporary religious preachers, the Buddha was the youngest and had the smallest congregation. According to the *Encyclopaedia of Religion and Ethics* (1910), a

12-volume work edited by James Hastings, Buddha lived five more years after Mahāvīra's death. According to the monks Kalyāṇa Vijayji and Vijayendra Sūrī, Mahāvīra attained liberation in 527 BCE.

Prominent Buddhist texts that mention the Buddha discussing Mahāvīra's Nirvāṇa include *Majjhima Nikāya-Sāmāgāma Sutta, Dīgha Nikāya - Pāsādika Sutta, Dīgha Nikāya - Sangītiparyāya Sutta.* Although Jacobi rejected these references because they are not mentioned in the last discourse of the Buddha, i.e. *Mahāparinibbāṇa Sutta*, the Buddhist references match precisely with the references in the Jain texts. Moreover, according to both Digambara and Śvētāmbara scholars, the *Śaka* calendar starts after six hundred five years and five months after the Nirvāṇa of Mahāvīra in 527 BCE.

HISTORICAL ANALYSIS OF THE YEARS OF THE BUDDHA'S AND MAHĀVĪRA'S NIRVĀṆA

Discussing the Buddha's Nirvāṇa, a distinguished historian, Gaurīśankara Hīrachanda Ojhā mentioned in his book *Bhāratīya Prāchīna Lipimālā:*

> The year of Buddha's Nirvana is not yet settled. In Sri Lanka, Myanmar, and Thailand, it is considered 544 BCE, which Assam's royal guru also accepts. In China, it is believed to be 638 BCE. The pioneering Chinese traveller Fāhyān mentioned that Buddha's Nirvana occurred 1497 years before he arrived in India in 400 CE, which comes to 1097 BCE. According to Dr Buhler, it is between 483-2 and 472-1 BCE; according to Prof. Kern, it is 388; according to Ferguson, it is 481 BCE; according to General Cunningham, it is 478 BCE; according to Max Müller, it is 477 BCE, according to Pundit Bhagavānlāla Inder, it is 638 BCE (quoting the text from Gayā), according to Miss Duff 477 BCE, according to Dr Bonnert, it is 483 BCE, according to Dr Fleet, it is 483 BCE, according to V.A. Smith, it is 486 or 487 BCE.

According to the book *Vīra Nirvāṇa Samvat Aur Jaina Kāla*

Gaṇanā by a Jain monk, Kalyāṇa Vijayajī, the Buddha was older than Mahāvīra by twenty years, and Mahāvīra's Nirvāṇa occurred fourteen years, five months and fifteen days after the Buddha's. Therefore, the Buddha's Nirvāṇa happened in 512 BCE. Xuanzang (Hiuen Tsang), who visited India in CE 630, mentioned, 'The Buddha lived for eighty years, and his Nirvana date is disputed. Different sects put the date in different full moon days of different months. Some say it happened 1200 years ago, some say 1500 years, and others say over nine hundred years.' According to a monk Nagarāja, Mahāvīra was older than the Buddha by seventeen years, and Buddha's Nirvāṇa occurred twenty-five years after Mahāvīra's. He cited Aśoka's inscriptions and the calendar calculations of the Buddha's life in Burmese and Tibetan traditions. Unfortunately, none of these settles the year of Buddha's Nirvāṇa.

Although Jain texts do not mention the Buddha's Nirvāṇa, there is a significant verse in the Hindu text *Bhāgavata Purāṇa* (1.6.24) that alludes to the Buddha's mother Ānjanī to be the daughter of King Anjan. The Burmese Buddhist tradition also mentions that the Buddha's maternal grandfather, Anjan, ruled in the Devadaha region. Anjan started the Burmese calendar in his name on Sunday, 17 February 648 BCE.[3] According to this calendar, the Buddha was born in the sixty-eighth year, renounced his worldly life in the ninety-sixth year, attained enlightenment in the hundred and third year, and attained Nirvāṇa in the hundred and forty-eighth year. Translating the Burmese calculations, M. Govind Pai concluded that the Buddha was born on Friday, 30 March 581 BCE, renounced on Monday, 18 June 553 BCE, attained enlightenment on Wednesday, 3 April 546 BCE, attained Nirvāṇa on Tuesday, 15 April 501 BCE.

Another Hindu text, *Vāyu Purāṇa*'s 170th verse, mentions that King Pradyot ruled for twenty-three years. According to the Tibetan tradition, Pradyot was born in the same year as the Buddha and started ruling in the same year the Buddha attained enlightenment. Since it is widely accepted that the Buddha attained enlightenment at thirty-five years of age, Pradyot was thirty-five when he was coronated as a king. He remained a king till he was fifty-eight. According to Jain tradition, Pradyot's son became the next king when Mahāvīra attained Nirvāṇa. The Buddha, who was the same age as Pradyot, must also have been fifty-eight when Mahāvīra passed away at the age of seventy-two. Therefore, the Buddha was born fourteen years after Mahāvīra. The Buddha's renunciation was around the time when Mahāvīra attained enlightenment. The Buddha's enlightenment was in the eighth year of Mahāvīra's omniscient phase. The Buddha passed away twenty-two years after Mahāvīra did. These years match *AC*'s calculations also. Pradyot was fourteen when Mahāvīra's parents passed away. Accordingly, considering 527 BCE to be Mahāvīra's final year, his birth year proves to be 599 BCE. Therefore, the Buddha's birth year is 585 BCE, and his final year is 505 BCE.

According to Janardan Bhatt, several Aśoka's inscriptions mention 256, which denotes the years since the Buddha's Nirvāṇa. Historians accept 269 BCE as the year when Aśoka was coronated as king. After eight years of his rule, he invaded Kalinga, but disgusted with the violence, he became a Buddhist follower. He propagated Dharma through inscriptions and by many other means for the next ten years, i.e. 249 BCE, 256 years after the Buddha's Nirvāṇa. Therefore, the Buddha's Nirvana year is proved to be 505 BCE.

NOTES

1. However, Herman Jacobi believed this place to be in the Śākya region, where the Buddha spent his last few days. A few other scholars, such as Rāhula Sānkṛtyāyana and Nāthurāma Premī, have disputed on similar lines.
2. *Journal of Bihar and Odisha Research Society*, 1-103

3. *Prabuddha Karnataka*, a Kannada quarterly published by the Mysore University, vol. XXVII (1945-6), no. 1, pp. 92-3. The Date of Nirvāṇa of Lord Mahavira in *Mahavira Commemoration Volume*, pp. 93-4 (cited in Hastīmal 1971: 779).

CHAPTER 5

Jainism, Dharma and Environmental Ethics

> Environmentalism is comparable to a child who only recently learned to walk. Ecospiritualities of different kinds are the invisible backbone of the growth of this child.
>
> SIGURD BERGMANN[1]

INTRODUCTION

Scholars such as Sigurd Bergmann have noted that each tradition is uniquely linked to its environment. It is best to investigate a native tradition for the ways each tradition or lineage absorbs the environment around it. On the contrary scholars such as John Cort have raised doubts about linking environment with religious traditions such as Jainism.[2] Given the absence of a formal category of environmental ethics in Jainism, this chapter explores Jainism's historical relationship to ecological ethics. I will also compare Jainism's perspectives on consuming natural resources with other lifestyles. From the few examples of Jain environmentalism, I also seek to redefine the categories such as 'religion' and 'environmental ethics', mainly as they are applied to the non-Western parts of the world, such as the Jains or Jainism.

Scholars of environmental ethics and Indic traditions have

differentiated two models of environmental awareness for India: the 'devotional model' and the 'renouncer model'. These two models are based on a long-standing dichotomy between the householders and ascetics.[3] Householders perform devotional and ritualistic activities, whereas ascetics perform austere practices. My research with the rural communities of Rajasthan and Gujarat suggests that their practices tend to be devotional rather than ascetic. To be sure, devout practitioners continue to attend discourses by ascetics and pay their respect to them. However, their practices primarily consist of daily rituals and *puja* at home and temples.[4] Fasting is another common practice performed by Indians. While lay Hindus eat fruits and vegetables during their fasts, lay Jains avoid water and all kinds of food.[5] This example indicates an interesting dimension of environmentalism inspired by Indian traditions. The two models of devotional and ascetic lead us into a dichotomy of the Hindu and Jain traditions. Most Hindu practitioners follow devotion in daily rituals. However, most Jain lay practitioners come much closer to the austere practices of ascetics. Jainism's role models are their Tīrthaṅkaras, who renounced all their belongings, including their clothing, to perform the toughest austerities possible. Even the temple-going Jains know that the Jain ideal is to renounce a householder life and to follow the path of their role models such as Mahāvīra, other Tīrthaṅkaras, and the contemporary monks and nuns.[6] The Jain ideal is to attain *Mokṣa*, liberation, by renouncing worldly life. In contrast, for most Hindus, especially the followers of Rāmānuja, Vallabha, and Chaitanya, the ideal is to become perfect devotees or attain *Mokṣa* by practising their routine householder lives, not by renouncing the householder life.

Scholars of Jain environmental ethics, such as Christopher Chapple, have advocated the ascetic model for ecological ethics in their writings. In contrast, scholars of Hindu environmental ethics, such as Vasudha Narayanan and David Haberman, have emphasised the devotional model. Both these models can contribute to preserving India's ecology. While the ascetic model can help reduce the over-exploitation of natural resources by limiting one's desire for more luxuries, the devotional model can help restore natural resources to their original beauty and harmony. The ascetic model can be prescribed for people of higher classes and developed societies, those who continue to plunder the planet for their extravagant consumption. Turning to the ascetic model, Chapple has advocated that non-violence to animals, trees and self, combined with non-possessiveness, can result in ecological awareness:[7]

> [T]he solutions that Gandhi proposed to counter the ills of colonialism can also be implemented to redress this new and ultimately deleterious situation. The observance of non-violence, coupled with a commitment to minimise the consumption of natural resources, can contribute to restoring and maintaining an ecological balance.

Chapple notes Gandhi as a role model who limited his possessions and 'vital needs' and thus can inspire environmental ethics. According to Chapple, Gandhi and others who follow ascetic and yogic values, such as truth, non-stealing, non-possession, celibacy and non-violence, serve as role models for limiting consumption and thus reducing the burden on ecology.[8] Chapple also notes that Jains, following their ascetic values, have exerted an active social conscience:[9]

> They successfully convinced the first Buddhist monks to cease their wanderings during the rainy season to avoid harm to the many insects and plants that sprout during the monsoons. The Jaina community has developed and implemented lay codes to integrate non-violent values into the workplace. Jainas have lobbied against nuclear weaponry. The head of the Terapanthi Shvetambara sect, Acharya Tulsi, took a public stance on numerous issues.

Against Lance Nelson's questioning of the world-negating

renouncer model, Eliot Deutsch observes,[10] 'Paradoxically, when nature is seen to be valueless in the most radical way, it can be made valuable with us in creative play.' Chapple's observations about the Jain community match Deutsch's argument that the practitioners of the ascetic traditions can also be proactive about ecological concerns.

Christopher Chapple recognised the dichotomy of the devotional or world-affirming model and ascetic or world-denying models of Indic traditions. He sought to see an underlying common theme in both in this way:[11]

> One model of Hindu spirituality encourages physicality through yoga practices that enhance the body's health and the senses' vitality. Other spiritual paths (such as Jainism) advocate renunciation of all sensual attachments to the world. However, even within the paths that relegate worldly concerns to a status of secondary importance, the doctrine of *dharma* emphasizes a need to act 'for the sake of the good of the world.' Particularly regarding such issues as the building of dams in the Narmada River Valley, this requires considering social ecology or the need to integrate environmental policy with the daily needs of tribal and other marginalized peoples.

Following Chapple's attempt to transcend the dichotomy of devotional and ascetic models, I want to further extend the notion of dharma by combining religion, ethics and ecology. One of the fundamental problems in studying or researching Indian traditions is the search for Western categories of knowledge within them. Scholars have long wrestled with various Western categories such as religion, ethics, theology, history and their Indian equivalents. Gerald Larson wrote about applying Indian categories of knowledge to studying India instead of looking for Western categories.[12] McKim Marriott's ethnosociology of India is rooted in the same philosophical problem.[13]

Strangely, the social sciences used in India today have developed from thoughts about Western rather than Indian cultural realities. As a result, although they pretend to have universal applicability, Western sciences often do not recognize and, therefore, cannot deal with the questions that many Indian institutions answer.

Elsewhere, Marriott notes that Western history has separated various knowledge domains such as religion, psychology, sociology, anthropology, and (if I may add, ethics and ecology). Still, scholars should not assume that non-Western cultures also wish to divide them. Following Marriott, I propose not to see environmentalism, ethics, or theology as separate categories in Indian traditions. I suggest that ethics, ecology and theology intertwine in Indian traditions as exemplified by various texts, recent movements and ethnographic encounters. I am posting this intertwined relationship in a 'dharmic' framework rather than a 'religious' one to stress the integration of ethics and theology in dharma or to avoid some specific incorrect connotation conveyed by the Western term religion.[14] Vijaya Nagarajan extends Karl Polanyi's understanding of embedded economies to that of embedded ecologies:[15]

> The prime reason for the absence of any concept of ecology is the difficulty of identifying ecological processes under conditions where they are embedded in non-ecological institutions. Ecological notions, beliefs, and practices are embedded in cultural forms, particularly religious and aesthetic practices and institutions.

I want to extend this 'embedded' notion further by combining ethics, ecology and theology with an overarching term, 'dharma', which is intertwined due to their varied interpretations. While it is true that environmentalism as a category does not exist in Indian traditions, it is equally valid that the dharmic Indian traditions have helped sustain the Indian ecology for several millennia by inspiring Indians to limit their needs. One of my students put it succinctly:

> What sets humans above beasts is their ability to cease or control

animal urges. Few animals can control eating, refuse to mate, or maintain their diet. This makes ascetics, fasting, celibacy, and vegetarianism (all essential Jain teachings and practices) fascinating to me (though not in my practice). India is the first place all these things occurred, making me think India may be the birthplace of humanity.

All Jain ascetics practice asceticism, fasting and celibacy. Similarly, the main diet of most Jains (and Hindus) primarily consists of rice, wheat, pulses and vegetables. In 2002, India's meat consumption was 3.78 kilograms per person, much less than other major meat-consuming regions.[16]

This shows that even after the advent of modernity and globalization, Indians have successfully preserved the vegetarian habits laid down by their dharmic traditions several millennia ago. Interestingly, meat-eating is now linked to climate change. In a groundbreaking 2006 report, the United Nations said that raising animals for food generates more greenhouse gases than all the cars and trucks combined. Senior UN Food and Agriculture Organization official Henning Steinfeld reported that the meat industry is 'one of the most significant contributors to today's most serious environmental problems'. As noted, we find a long tradition of avoiding meat in Indian dietary habits, as if already assuming the latest reports from the UN mention that meat eating is one of the main reasons for climate change. Even after Western media reported[17] the connection of meat eating with climate change, leading environmentalists such as Al Gore, who received the Nobel Prize for his work in this regard, failed to notice meat consumption in Western society's food habits.[18]

Western society and environmentalists like Gore have ignored such clear evidence. Thomas Friedman, a leading columnits at *The New York Times*, noted this and rejected any changes needed in the Western lifestyle even while demanding 'greener' initiatives from the US government (*The New York*

Times, 15 April 2007). This Western dichotomy between expecting the 'environmentalist' initiatives from the governments and businesses *without* changing personal lifestyles was the subject of the conclusion of Ramachandra Guha's book with an appropriate title, *How Much Should a Person Consume?'* Guha observes that Western society consists of 20 per cent of the world but consumes about 80 per cent of the world's production. The rest of the world, composed of 80 per cent of the world's population, consumes only about 20 per cent of the world's output. Guha agrees with conservationist Ashish Kothari and criticizes the 'hypocrisy' of the developed world:[19]

> It is the *allegedly civilized* who have decimated forests and the wildlife that previously sustained both tiger and tribal. With rifles and quest for trophies, [they] first hunted wild species to extinction; now [they] disguise [themselves] as conservationists and complain that adivasis are getting in the way. The actual 'population problem' is in America, where the birth of one child has the same impact on the global environment as the birth of about seventy Indonesian children. Worse, the birth of an American dog or cat was the ecological equivalent of the birth of a dozen Bangladeshi children.

With social activism based on dharmic traditions such as Buddhism and Jainism, inspired and founded by the Buddha and Mahāvīra, Indian society had successfully moved away from animal sacrifices and killings in the Vedic era to lifestyles based on vegetarianism. Jainism classifies the various living beings under different grades according to their development and sense faculties – under two broad classes, *trasa* or mobile and *sthāvara* or immobile. *Trasa* beings possess two, three, four, and five sense organs. *Sthāvara* beings have only one sense organ of touch, and they are of five kinds: earth-bodied, water-bodied, fire-bodied, air-bodied, and vegetables. A Jain monk is supposed to avoid injury to all *trasa* and *sthāvara* beings. A Jain householder should also prevent injury to *trasa* beings and minimize injury to *sthāvara* beings. Therefore, Jain householders avoid eating meat and vegetables that are roots or trunks of plants. They also avoid eating fruits and vegetables containing living organisms like figs and honey. This emphasis on vegetarianism can be linked with less meat consumption in Indian society, as I showed above.

Ironically, scholars have primarily ignored vegetarianism as one of the essential dharmic lessons inspired by an Indian tradition that can significantly help reduce climate change. We can similarly note others, such as *Aparigraha* (non-accumulation), which have continued to be an 'obstacle' to the consumerist revolution in India. Only in the 1990s did India finally start embracing the Western capitalist model of the economy, and now market forces are fast transcending the proverbial 'Hindu rate of economic growth'. Until this Western market invasion, this growth rate might have been the result and the reason for limited Indian spending on consumer goods.[20]

Valmik Thapar connects Indian traditions to ecology in this way,

> [A] Fifty years after independence, the Indian subcontinent can still be justly proud of its enormously varied flora and fauna. In India alone, 13,000 flowering plants and 65,000 fauna species have been recorded, including 2,000 fish, 1,200 birds, and 340 mammals. There are numerous species of reptiles and amphibians, including turtles, crocodiles, and over a hundred species of frogs and toads. India is also the only place in the world with lions and tigers. While the extremes of climate and habitat explain the enormous diversity of life, they do not explain how this wealth of flora and fauna has managed to survive on such an immensely crowded continent. Despite all the pressures, the diversity of flora and fauna is *the richest in the world*. The answer lies, at least, in the special relationship that the people of the subcontinent had, and continue to have, with the other living creatures that share their land. *This unique relationship is inextricably linked to religion*. Despite the influx of cable television

and Western consumerism, religion is still significant in rural life. Hinduism treats many animals and birds with respect. Reverence for things natural also extends to trees and plants.[21]

Thapar, like most English-speaking Indians, uses the word 'religion' to describe a rural way of life, but what he is describing is the daily 'way of life', which includes ethics, morality, duties, law, and 'religion'. In my observations, Indians describe these categories by their everyday vernacular term dharma or dharam. In the following section, I note some examples of Jain environmental activism that reflect their dharma. I also note the potential of Jainism's interaction and influence with the Bishnoi community, founded in fifteenth-century Rajasthan.

BISHNOI COMMUNITY AND JAINISM

Although the Bishnoi community considers itself a caste group within the larger Hindu community, several social and cultural practices match Jain communities. Bishnoi Guru Jambheśvara, in the fifteenth-century Rajasthan, was the first Indian guru to emphasise ecological awareness in his teachings. His twenty-nine rules expressly prohibited harming trees or animals and encouraged vegetarianism. Of his twenty-nine rules, eight rules were prescribed to preserve and promote animal husbandry. These include the non-sterilisation of bulls and keeping the male goats in a sanctuary, the prohibition against killing the animals, cutting down any green trees, and providing protection to all life forms. The followers are even directed to see the firewood devoid of small insects before burning it in their hearths. The Bishnoi emphasis on revering the animals and trees resembles Hindu rituals and Jainism's emphasis on non-violence.

Although Jambheśvara prohibited keeping goats as pets, he ordained against the slaughter of goats and sheep in another verse, *Kinnri tharpi chhali roso kinnri Gadar gai, sool chubhijey karak duheli to hai jayo jeeva no ghai,* which means by whose sanction do butchers kill sheep and goats? Since even a prick by a thorn is extremely painful to human beings, is it proper to indulge in those killings? Therefore, these animals should be treated as their kith and kin and should not be harmed in any way. In another verse, while preaching to another disciple Nathaji, Jambheśvara says, *Chhery bheri adi ko par upkari mann, raksha main tatpar rahey so buddhiman* that means that goats, sheep, etc., are rendering services to others, and the one who protects them is a wise person. As a rule, following the Holi festival, villagers participate in a public auction to take care of the cattle sanctuary for the following year.

Based on the similarities between the two non-violent traditions of Jainism and Bishnois, it is unsurprising that a noted conservationist, Valmik Thapar, called the Bishnoi tradition an 'offshoot of Jainism' (1997). In my quest to explore their potential relationship, I noticed another similarity between the Bishnoi and the Jain traditions. Although most Jains perform rituals in temples with elaborate images, a new sect emerged on the borders of Rajasthan and Gujarat that rejected any use of images like Jambheśvara's rejection in the Bishnoi tradition during the same time. The new Jain sect was founded by Lonka Shah, born in the Sirohi district in South-West Rajasthan in 1418 and died in 1484,[22] while Jambheśvara lived from 1452 to 1537. Lonka Shah's movement to reject image worship started in 1452 and became widespread in Rajasthan and Gujarat by 1474. The manuscripts found in Bikaner and Nagore, towns near the birthplace of Jambheśvara indicate this. Like the twenty-nine rules given by Jambheśvara for Bishnois, Lonka Shah's written work is also listed with numerical titles, '34 Statements', 'Basket of 58 Statements', and '13 Questions and Their Answers'. He was believed to have about four hundred ascetic disciples and thousands of lay followers. Out of forty-five people who took initiation under him simultaneously, Lakhamsiji, Nunaji, Shobhaji, Dungarsiji, and Bhaninji became prominent monastic leaders and eventually established their sanghas after the death of Lonka Shah and named them as different branches of Lokagachha. Eventually, one branch became a distinguished branch of the Sthānakavāsī sect called Nagori, which developed in the Nagore town of Rajasthan, the birthplace of Jambheśvara. Given the wandering nature of Sthānakavāsī ascetics and the powerful new movement launched by Lonka Shah, it can be speculated that Jambheśvara may have met one of the followers or disciples of Lonka Shah that led him to develop the Bishnoi code of conduct based on non-iconic rituals and non-violence towards animals.

In my fieldwork, I visited the Bishnoi cattle shelter institution Shri Jagatguru Jambheśvara Goshala Sanstha at Mukam. This institution takes care of about thirteen hundred and thirty five, and their food is brought from Haryana and Punjab. About 8,000 to 9,000 kilograms of food is fed to them daily. Amar That inspires this institution, an animal shelter institution mentioned in one of the verses by Jambheśvara's disciple Udoji Naina, *Bakra paley that kar, tanni nahin nakho,* which means that the goats should be looked after in sanctuaries and bullocks should not be castrated. Jains have also long supported such institutions in different parts of India, and I visited one of the cattle shelter institutions described below.

EXAMPLES OF NON-VIOLENT ENVIRONMENTALISM

According to Ramavtar Aggarwal, secretary of the All-India Goshala Federation, there are more than three thousand Goshalas in India, and the Sumati Center at Pavapuri is one of the biggest in India.[23] Another organisation called Love4Cow maintains a nationwide list of Goshalas maintained by Jains (and Hindus) and lists more than six hundred and seventy Goshalas in Rajasthan alone. Though not trained as a scholar of Jain tradition, Michael Tobias recognised a commonality between his environmental interests and the Jain worldview.[24] Similar Hindu and Jain community efforts are widely reported in many places in India.[25] *The Hindu* reported a Jain/Hindu Goshala Satyam Shivam Sundaram Gaunivas at Gaganpahad near Hyderabad (5 July 2005). Considered South India's biggest cow shelter and managed by the Shiv Mandir Goshala set up by jeweller-turned-philanthropist Dharam Raj Ranka, the shelter houses over two thousand cows rescued from slaughterhouses and three hundred and two hundred bulls. Justice Gumanmal Lodha, a Jain ex-lawmaker from Rajasthan, published a detailed report to ban cow slaughter in India during his tenure as chairperson of the National Commission on Cattle and submitted it to the Union Government of India. In four volumes, the report called for stringent laws to protect the cow and its progeny in the interest of India's rural economy. Lodha moved close to a national ban on cow slaughter in India, although most states except Kerala have already banned it long ago. However, this political activism is also interpreted as pseudo-environmentalism since it is tied with a more significant motive of luring the 'Hindu' vote banks in the electoral politics of Indian democracy.

Another dimension of Jain principles in practice is evident at the Jain Bird Hospital in Delhi at the Digambar Jain Temple, opposite Red Fort near Chandni Chowk, where the patients admitted are only birds, preferably the vegetarian ones. Prachin Shri Aggarwal Digambar Jain Panchayat established it in 1956 on the Jain principle of aversion to killing. The hospital has separate wards in cages for different species, like sparrows, parrots, domestic fowls, and pigeons. It also has a research laboratory and an intensive care unit for severe patients. The nearby people, especially the Jain merchants, bring the birds for treatment, usually wounded by fowlers, ceiling fans, or other means. The hospital admits a maximum of sixty injured birds daily and about 15,000 annually. They are treated, bathed, and fed a nutritious diet for fast recovery. Later, the birds are free from the hospital's terrace overlooking the Red Fort. To show another example of Jains protecting the animals, in 1969, Goa's largest wildlife sanctuary was named after Mahāvīra. The Governor at the time was a Jain, who suggested the name. In 1982, the local Jains donated Rs. 12.5 million for the development of the sanctuary.[26]

Another newer orchard, 'Tapovan Ashram', is in the denuded forests and hill region of the Aravallis at Naya Kheda village in the Udaipur district.[27] This is a lush green garden of about 15 acres with a high-water table and exotic herbs and fruits. This began as an experiment by a Jain horticulturist, Ratan Chand Mehta, in 1991. He harvested the rainwater from the nearby hills, and soon, the water table of that small area was higher than the surrounding areas. The farming here is titled *Bhagwan Bharose Mast Kheti* (God Blessed Biodiverse Farming). I asked Mehta about his inspiration for the Ashram (Personal communication, 17 June 2007). He emphasized his Jain background and mentioned the *Ācārāṅga Sūtra*, one of the earliest texts that recorded Mahāvīra's teachings. Christopher Chapple also cites *Ācārāṅga Sūtra* (2.4.2.11–12), in which Mahāvīra tells his disciples to recognise trees' inherent value and turn their thoughts from materiality by reflecting on the beauty of sparing a tree from human exploitation. Sadhvi Shilapi also cites from *Ācārāṅga Sūtra* (1.1.5) to show that Mahāvīra proclaims that anyone who neglects or disregards the existence of earth, air, water and vegetation disregards his existence that is intrinsically bound up with them.[28]

Continuing my description of the environmentalism of Jain organisations, JAINA (an umbrella organisation of several Jain associations in North America) has a Jivadaya Committee (Committee for the Compassion for All Beings) that has selected about a dozen animal shelter organisations in India. JAINA encourages its Jain members to send donations to these organisations to help fund India's animal shelter and protection activities. In 2003, Nitin Talsania, an active member of several JAINA committees in New Jersey, helped the Voith Family of Angelica, New York, in their struggle to raise cows following their Hindu practice.[29] Similarly, the Jain Center of Southern California joined with 'The Purple Cow and Friends', a nonprofit organisation near San Diego. Its director, Ms. Tiffany, and her co-workers collected fruits, vegetables and grain from local farmers and grocery stores for over one hundred animals (including cows, dogs, pigs, goats, horses and birds).[30]

In July 2007, at the fourteenth biennial JAINA convention in New Jersey, I met Saurabh Dalal, president of the Vegetarian Society of the District of Columbia, the oldest vegetarian society in the USA. Inspired by his Jain background of *ahimsa* and non-violence, Saurabh has spread awareness about the connection between a meat-based diet and climate change. I attended his talk at the convention, where he presented several interesting facts. A vegetarian diet requires only 10 per cent of the land that the standard meat-based diet does, while a vegan diet would require only 5 per cent of the same land. Similarly, by becoming vegan, one can save 3,900 gallons of water.[31] I also met a Jain activist, Pravin K. Shah, who became a strict vegan after visiting a dairy where he saw the cruel treatment of cattle there. Anne Vallely argues that Jains in the North American diaspora have shifted from India's conservative and orthodox Jain community.[32] She notes that most Jains in India are not so active in social and ecological areas, whereas the 'diaspora' Jains, especially the second-generation youth, are active in interfaith and animal welfare forums and groups. However, my observations from the fieldwork in India differ from her conclusions. In my animal welfare and protection case studies, the Jain community and other communities in India have taken an active role. This also matches the observation of Peter Flugel, who notes the 'sociocentric' role of the Jain community in India.[33]

Jain history is full of examples, legends, and tales of protecting and avoiding injury to plants, animals, and the environment in general.[34] Jains believed that the nineteenth Jain Tīrthaṅkara Mallinātha had taken responsibility for protecting the forests. During the reign of the Mughal emperor Akbar, a prominent Jain monk, Hiravijaya Suri, was invited by the royal court through the Governor of Gujarat. Following the Jain tradition, Hiravijaya Suri walked on foot to Fatehpur Sikari, where he first met the Muslim scholar Abul Fazal and then Akbar. He influenced Akbar to issue several ordinances in CE 1592 to prohibit animal slaughter for six months, to present the Shatrunjaya Temple to Jain authorities, to stop confiscating the property of a dead person, to stop taxes against non-Muslims, and to liberate the prisoners. Even fishing was prohibited in Fatehpur Sikri during his time. This is evident from an edict of CE 1593 found at the eastern entrance hall of Adinatha Temple at Shatrunjaya written by Hemavijay. Akbar also refrained from eating meat for a certain period of the year.

CONCLUSION

There are several examples of Jains actively protecting plants, animals, birds and the environment in general. Still, it is true that, like other traditional societies, Jains (and other Indians) have yet to wake up to the problems of environmental disasters. Most sects, castes and other conventional Indian groups continue to practice their dharmic rituals without being mindful of the ecological connections. Yet, despite being the second most populated country on the planet, India continues to boast of the richest flora and fauna. This bio-diversity has been preserved for thousands of years, as noted by Thapar above.

If ecological awareness is translated into a dharmic message, it will remain a distant voice primarily limited to armchair exercises in political or scholarly discussions. For most Indians who speak, think and read in vernacular frameworks, terms such as 'climate change' or 'biodiversity' have limited appeal. Thus, the rhetoric based on these terms will have limited appeal. The sooner these textual and intellectual exercises become widespread practical movements, the better for our endangered planet. Sustainable, need-based usage of natural resources has sustained our planet for thousands of years, not the greedy exploitation we have done in the last few centuries in our drive for modern luxuries and comforts. Historically, the population and consumption of natural resources of Asian civilizations have always been much higher than that of Western cultures. Yet, the Westernised notion of progress in the last few centuries has endangered our planet.[35] Unless we reform and expand our idea of progress by mixing ideas and concepts from the local communities, all ecological rhetoric will remain insignificant for the traditional communities worldwide.

NOTES

1. Sigurd Bergmann, *Ecotheology*, vol. 11.3, September 2006.
2. John Cort, 'Green Jainism? Notes and Queries toward a Possible Jain Environment Ethic', in *Jainism and Ecology: Nonviolence in the Web of Life*, ed. Christopher Key Chapple. Cambridge: Harvard University Press, 2002.
3. Pankaj Jain, 'Householders and Renouncers, The Holistic Combination in Indian Thought', in *Studies in Vedanta: Essays in Honor of S. S. Rama Rao Pappu*, ed. P. George Victor and V.V.S.

Saibaba, New Delhi: D.K. Printworld, 2006, pp. 165-80.

4. T.N. Madan, *Non-Renunciation: Themes and Interpretations of Hindu Culture.* New York: Oxford University Press, 1996.
5. Padmanabh S. Jaini, *The Jaina Path of Purification.* Berkeley: University of California Press, 1979, pp. 157-85.
6. Anne Vallely, *Guardians of the Transcendent: Ethnography of a Jain Ascetic Community.* Toronto; Buffalo: University of Toronto Press, 2002b.
7. Christopher Key Chapple, *Nonviolence to Animals, Earth, and Self in Asian Traditions.* Albany: SUNY Press, 1993, p. 73.
8. Ibid., p. 71.
9. Nancy M. Martin and Joseph Runzo (eds.), *Ethics in the World Religions.* Oxford: Oneworld, 2001.
10. E. Deutsch, 'A Metaphysical Grounding for Natural Reverence, East-West', in J.B. Callicott and R. Ames (eds.), *Nature in Asian Traditions of Thought: Essays in Environmental Philosophy*, Albany: SUNY Press, 1989, p. 264.
11. Christopher Key Chapple, 'Hinduism, Jainism and Ecology', in *Earth Ethics,* vol. 10, no. 1, Fall 1998.
12. Gerald Larson, 'A Beautiful Sunset . . . Mistaken for Dawn', Some Reflections on Religious Studies, India Studies, and the Modern University', in *Journal of American Academy of Religion* (72/4), 2004, pp. 1003-20.
13. McKim Marriott (ed.), *India Through Hindu Categories,* New Delhi: Sage, 1990, p. 1.
14. Although this is not how everyone in the West sees it and the categories in the Western academy result less from a deliberate separation, than from a problem in doctoral studies which rewards expertise in highly focused research areas. And recently, Interdisciplinary studies are on the rise thus diluting the hard-wired categories of the past.
15. Vijaya Nagarajan, 'Embedded Ecology', in *Purifying the Earthly Body of God: Religion and Ecology in Hindu India*, ed. Lance Nelson. Albany: SUNY Press, 1998, pp. 165-195.
16. https://ourworldindata.org/grapher/daily-meat-consumption-per-person (accessed on 20 February 2019).

17. Such as *CNN, Fox News, The New York Times, Time Magazine, Guardian* (UK), and *Telegraph* (UK). See for example, mean guzzler in *The New York Times*, 28 January 2008.
18. http://blog.peta.org/archives/al_gore/ (viewed on 20 December 2007).
19. Ramachandra Guha, *How Much Should a Person Consume? Environmentalism in India and the United States*. Berkeley: University of California, 2006, p. 149.
20. 'Story, Ritual, and Environment in Rajasthan', in *Sacred Landscapes and Cultural Politics: Planting a Tree,* ed. Philip P. Arnold and Ann Grodzins Gold. Aldershot: Ashgate, 2001.
21. Valmik Thapar, *Land of the Tiger, A Natural History of the Indian Subcontinent*. Berkeley: University of California Press, 1997.
22. Sagarmal Jain and Vijay Kumar. *Sthanakwasi Jain Parampara ka Itihasa.* Varanasi: Parshvanatha Vidyapitha, 2003.
23. According to the center's mission, 'Animals in this shelter get all the love and affection and are taken care of, like a mother who loves and cares for her children selflessly and teaches them all about their traditions. The center has statues of divine beings that provide the animals with spiritual ambience. The sacred Jain Navkar Mantra is played throughout the day in the shelter that transforms it into a center of divine presence. Food for the cattle is prepared according to the Jain beliefs of sanctity and purity. This includes green grass, hay, nutritious cattle food, oil, jaggary, invigorating sweets, pulses, etc. The center also maintains a bird shelter where birds are taken care of.'
24. Michael Tobias, *Life Force: The World of Jainism.* Fremont: Asian Humanities Press, 1991.
25. Deryck O. Lodrick, *Sacred Cows, Sacred Places: Origins and Survivals of Animal Homes in India*. Berkeley: University of California Press, 1981.
26. I thank Shonil Bhagwat at the Oxford Long-Term Ecology Laboratory, for this information (personal communication).
27. www.tapovanashram.com (viewed on 15 June 2007) 'It is based on the Mahayana philosophy of "nothingness" of Gautam Buddha. It corresponds closely to nature and the laws of nature

such as the unity of everything, co-existence, self-regulation and regeneration, interdependence of each entity, and is a definite shift from object to relationships. It dwells on the basic premise that the universe is a living co-existential creative experience where the smallest micro-organism (microcosm) is intricately interwoven with the entire cosmos (cosmo-vision) and that the systems thinking is contextual environmental thinking. Pure natural farming albeit God blessed bio-diverse farming which we have preferred to call "Bhagwan Bharose Mast Kheti" (or non-farming) is deeply articulated in the ways of living and farming of the tribal community of the south Rajasthan of Aravallis Hill region. It is dependent on the blessings of God in terms of the monsoon rains, all powerful source of energy, the sunshine, unpolluted free air and the bio-diverse plant and animal world which has a tremendous capacity to adapt itself to all kinds of environmental conditions. It is "Mast" because there is no worry as to the yield, income, or profit per acre of land or per person deflecting the modern concepts of growth or progress. A mixed pattern of tree, shrub and herb species, one over the other, can take care of the food, fuel, fiber, fodder, resin, gum, medicinal herbs, for abundant health and wealth needed for a frugal and self-fulfilling living. The main features of 'Bhagwan Bharose Mast' farming are minimal human intervention, least land manipulation, zero or (minimum) tillage, least use of machine and fossil fuel energy, no use of chemical fertilizers, no use of chemical pesticides (except herbal formulations), herbicides, etc., rain fed, lifesaving irrigation may sometimes be needed, multi-tier bio-diverse mixed farming including true, shrub and herb species to meet the diverse needs of food, fiber, fuel, oils, gums and medicinal plants, being purely natural, strategies based on watershed area delineation converging in common rain water outlet following soil and water conservation, recharge and recycling techniques, developing institutional, human and material resources to restore the human disturbed eco-system to bring it to earlier pristine forms.'

28. Christopher Key Chapple, *Jainism and Ecology: Nonviolence in the*

Web of Life. Cambridge: Harvard University Press, 2002, p. 160.

29 http://www.nomoreinjustice.org/media_articles_cowscantcomehome.htm (viewed on 3 May 2007).

30. http://www.jainworld.com/society/jainevents/GJE2003/Purple%20Cow%20Animal%20shelter.htm (viewed on 5 May 2007).

31. Such arguments are vindicated by the latest study by the National Institute of Livestock and Grassland Science in Tsukuba, Japan (*Telegraph*, UK, 23 July 2007). Similar conclusions were reached by Gidon Eshel and Pamela Martin, assistants of geophysics at the University of Chicago (*ABC News*, 19 April 2006).

32. Anne Vallely, 'From Liberation to Ecology: Ethical Discourses among Orthodox and Diaspora Jains', in Christopher Key Chapple, ed., *Jainism and Ecology: Nonviolence in the Web of Life.* Cambridge: Harvard University Press, 2002a.

33. Peter Flugel, Review of *Jainism and Ecology: Non-Violence in the Web of Life*, ed. Christopher Key Chapple. Environmental Ethics 27, no. 2. (2005), 201.

34. Christopher Key Chapple, Jainism and Nonviolence', in *Subverting Hatred: The Challenge of Nonviolence in Religious Traditions*, ed. Daniel Smith-Christopher. Boston: Boston Research Center for the 21st Century, 1998. pp. 13-24.

35. Ramachamdra Guha, *How Much Should a Person Consume? Environmentalism in India and the United States*, Berkeley: University of California, 2006, p. 5.

Bibliography

ABBREVIATIONS

AC	*Āvaśyaka Chūrṇi*
AN	*Āvaśyaka Niryukti*
AS	*Āchārānga Sūtra*
BS	*Bhagavatī Sūtra*
BS	*2 Bhagavatī Śataka*
BKB	*Bṛhat Kalpa Bhāṣya*
KS	*Kalpa Sūtra*
SK	*Sūtra Kṛtāṅga*
TSPC	*Triśaṣti Śalākā Puruṣa Caritra*
UDS	*Upāsaka Daśā Sūtra*
VS	*Vipāka Sūtra*

SOURCES IN GUJARATI, HINDI, PRAKRIT, AND SANSKRIT

Bhadrabāhu. 1981. *Āvaśyaka Niryukti*, with Haribhadra's commentary, Vol. 1. Bombay: Āgamodaya Samiti.

Bhārill, Hukamchand. 1976. *Vītrāgī Vyaktitva Bhagvāna Mahāvīra*. Jaipur: Pt Todarmal Smarak Trust.

Gaṇī, Kalyaṇvijayjī. 2002. *Śramaṇa Bhagvāna Mahāvīra*. Ahmedabad: Shardaben Chimanbhai Educational Research Centre.

Hastīmal, Āchārya. 1971. *Jain Dharma Kā Maulika Itihāsa: Part 1*. Jaipur: Jain Itihāsa Samiti.

Jacobi, Hermann. 1879. *Kalpasutra of Bhadrabahu*. Leipzig: Commission bei F.A. Brockhaus.

Jain, Balbhadra. 1974. *Jain Dharma Kā Prāchīna Itihāsa*. Delhi: Rajasthani Printing Agency.

———. 1998. "Vaiśālī-Kundagrām." *Prākṛt Vidyā* 9 (4): 17–24.

Jain, Jagdishchandra. 1945. *Mahāvīra Vardhamāna*. Allahabad: Law Journal Press.

———. 1977. *Bhagwāna Mahāvīra*. New Delhi: National Book Trust.

Jain, Kamta Prasad. 1924. *Bhagwāna Mahāvīra*. Surat: Digambara Jaina Pustakālaya.

Jain, Virendra. 2009. *Anuttara Yogī: Tīrthaṅkara Mahāvīra*. New Delhi: Bhāratīya Jñānapīṭha.

Jambūvijaya, Muni (ed.) 1978. *Āyāraṅga-Suttam*. Delhi: Agamodaya Samiti.

Jinadāsa. 1928–29. *Āvaśyaka Cūrṇi*. Vols. 1–2. Ratlam: Publisher unknown. https://jainelibrary.org/, accessed on April 1, 2019.

Jinasena. 2003. *Ādi Purāṇa*. Edited and translated by Pannalal Jain. Vols. 1–2. New Delhi: Bhāratīya Jñānapīṭha.

Mishra, Yogendra. 1954. "Mahāvīra Kī Janmabhūmi Vaiśālī." In *Chandābāī Abhinandan Granth*, 669–676. Patna: Indian Nation Press.

Puṇyavijaya, Muni, and A. M. Bhojak, (eds.) 1977. *Āvaśyakasūtra in Dasaveyāliyasuttam, Uttarajjhayaṇāiṃ and Āvassayasuttaṃ*. Bombay: Jaina Āgama Series 15.

———. 1962. *Pauma Chariyam*. Varanasi: Prakrit Text Society.

Ṛṣi, Amolak. 1949. *Jambudweep Prajñapti*. Secunderabad: Śāstrodhāra Mudrālaya.

Shastri, Manoharlal. 1917. *Mahāvīra Purāṇa*. Bombay: Jain Granth Uddharak Karyalaya.

Shastri, Navinchandra. 1954. "Mahāvīra Kā Bodhi Sthāna." In *Chandābāī Abhinandan Granth*, 649–651. Patna: Indian Nation Press.

Surī, Guṇachandra. 1929. *Śrī Mahāvīra Charitam*. Bombay: Jivanchand Jain Pustakoddhara Javeri Bazar.

SOURCES IN ENGLISH

Andersen, Ross. 2019. "A Journey into the Animal Mind: What Science Can Tell Us About How Other Creatures Experience the World." *The Atlantic*. https://www.theatlantic.com/magazine/archive/2019/03/what-the-crowknows/580726/, accessed on May 10, 2019.

Aquique, Md. 1978. "Mithila—The Heart of Jainism." *Jain Journal*, 12 (4): 126–131.

Armstrong, Karen. 2002. *Buddha*. London: Penguin.

Burnell, Arthur Coke. 1875. *On the Aindra School of Sanskrit Grammarians: Their Place in Sanskrit and Subordinate Literatures*. India: Basel Mission Book & Tract Depository.

Campbell, Joseph. 2020. *The Hero with a Thousand Faces*. Los Angeles: Joseph Campbell Foundation.

Chapple, Christopher Key. 2002. *Jainism and Ecology: Nonviolence in the Web of Life*. Cambridge, Cambridge: Harvard University Press.

Chattopadhyaya, B. K. 1953. *Kalpa Sūtra*. Calcutta: The University of Calcutta.

Coward, Harold G. 1985. *Jung and Eastern Thought*. Albany: State University of New York Press.

Davidson, Cliff I. 1979. "Air Pollution in Pittsburgh: A Historical Perspective." *Journal of the Air Pollution Control Association*, 29 (10): 1035–1041.

Dhammika, Venerable Shravasti. 1993. *The Edicts of King Asoka: An English Rendering*. Kandy: Buddhist Publication Society.

Doniger, Wendy. 1993. *Purāṇa Perennis: Reciprocity and Transformation in Hindu and Jaina Texts*. Albany: State University of New York Press.

Dundas, Paul. 2002. *The Jains*. London: Routledge.

______. 2020. "Pārśva and Mahāvīra in History." In *Brill's Encyclopedia of Jainism Online*, John E. Cort, Paul Dundas, Knut A. Jacobsen and Kristi L. Wiley (eds.). Leiden: Brill.

Dumézil, Georges. 1988. Trans. D. Coltman. *Mitra-Varuna: An Essay on Two Indo-European Representations of Sovereignty* (2nd edition). New York: Zone Books.

Flügel, Peter. 2005. Review of *Jainism and Ecology: Nonviolence in the Web of Life*, Christopher Key Chapple (ed.). *Environmental Ethics*, 27 (2): 201.

Gandhi, S. L. 2015. *Acharya Mahapragya: A Journey to Wisdom*. Noida: Harper Element.

Greendex. 2009. https://www.nationalgeographic.com/greendex/assets/GS_NGS_Full_Report_May09.pdf, accessed on April 6, 2019.

Guha, Ramachandra. 2006. *How Much Should a Person Consume? Environmentalism in India and the United States*. Berkeley: University of California Press.

Helton, Tim. 2007. "Mahāvīra, Mohandas, and Martin: An Ancient Religion's Influence on the United States Civil Rights Movement." Unpublished paper.

Heesterman, J. C. 1985. *The Inner Conflict of Tradition: Essays in Indian Ritual, Kinship, and Society*. Chicago: University of Chicago Press.

Jacobi, Hermann. 1884. *Sacred Books of the East - Section 22*. Oxford: Oxford University Press.

Jain, Manoj. 2003. *Mahāvīra: The Hero of Nonviolence*. New Delhi: Penguin Books.

Jain, Pankaj. 2011. "Jainism, Dharma, and Environmental Ethics." *Union Seminary Quarterly Review*, 61 (1): 121–135.

______. 2016. *Dharma and Ecology of Hindu Communities: Sustenance and Sustainability*. London: Routledge.

______. 2019. *Dharma in America: A Short History of Hindu-Jain Diaspora*. London: Routledge.

———. 2023. *Modern Jainism: A Historical Approach*. Singapore: Springer.

Jaini, M. C. 1908. *Life of Mahāvīra*. Allahabad: The Indian Press.

Jaini, Padmanabh S. 1977. "Jina Ṛṣabha as an 'Avatāra' of Viṣṇu." *Bulletin of the School of Oriental and African Studies*, 40 (2): 321–337.

———. 1979. *The Jaina Path of Purification*. Delhi: Motilal Banarsidass.

———. 1991. "Values in Comparative Perspective: Svadharma versus Ahiṃsā." In *Collected Papers on Buddhist Studies*, 155–166. Delhi: Motilal Banarsidass.

Johnson, Helen M. 1931. *Trishashti Shalaka Purusha Caritra*. Vadodara: Oriental Institute.

King, Mary. 1999. *Mahatma Gandhi and Martin Luther King Jr: The Power of Nonviolent Action (Cultures of Peace)*. Paris: UNESCO.

Koneswaran, Gowri, and Danielle Nierenberg. 2008. "Global Farm Animal Production and Climate Change: Impacting and Mitigating Climate Change." *Environmental Health Perspectives*, 116 (5): 578–582.

Kragh, U. T. 2011. "Personal Biography in Jaina Literature." *Śramaṇa*, 62 (1): 103–127.

Lakshmi, Rama. 2009. "Son Marks Martin Luther King's 1959 Visit to India." *The Washington Post*, February 18, 2009.

Lal, Vinay. 2000. "Too Deep for Deep Ecology: Gandhi and the Ecological Vision of Life." In *Hinduism and Ecology: The Intersection of Earth, Sky, and Water*, Christopher Key Chapple and Mary Evelyn Tucker (eds.), 183-212. Cambridge, MA: Harvard University Press.

Larson, Gerald. 2004. "'A Beautiful Sunset...Mistaken for Dawn': Some Reflections on Religious Studies, India Studies, and the Modern University." *Journal of the American Academy of Religion*, 72 (4): 1003–1020.

Law, B. C. 1936. *Mahāvīra: His Life and Teachings*. London: Luzac & Co.

Lodrick, Deryck O. 1981. *Sacred Cows, Sacred Places: Origins and Survivals of Animal Homes in India*. Berkeley: University of California Press.

Long, Jeffery D. 2008. *Jainism: An Introduction*. London: I.B. Tauris.

Maharaj, C. 1942. *Bhagwan Mahavir*. Translated by Ramchandra Sharma (1st edition). Ratlam: Jainoday Pustak Prakashan Samiti.

Marriott, McKim, ed. 1990. *India through Hindu Categories*. New Delhi: Sage Publications.

Mora, Camilo, Derek P. Tittensor, Sina Adl, Alastair G. B. Simpson, and Boris Worm. 2011. "How Many Species Are There on Earth and in the Ocean?" *Public Library of Science* Biology 9 (8): n.p.

Murcott, Susan. 2006. *First Buddhist Women: Poems and Stories of Awakening*. Berkeley: Parallax Press.

Nojeim, Michael J. 2004. *Gandhi and King: The Power of Nonviolent Resistance*. Westport: Praeger.

Olivelle, Patrick. 2004. *Manu Smṛti: Manu's Code of Law: A Critical Edition and Translation of the Mānava-Dharmaśāstra*. New York: Oxford University Press.

Pals, Daniel L. 2022. *Ten Theories of Religion*. New York: Oxford University Press.

Raghavachari, S. n.d. *Mahāvīra: His Life and Teachings*. Bhavnagar: Jain Sastu Sāhitya.

Rotman, Michael. 2010. "Cuyahoga River Fire." *Cleveland Historical*. https://clevelandhistorical.org/items/show/63, accessed on April 6, 2019.

Sino-Indian Studies. 1945. Vol. 1. Kolkata: China Press Limited.

Shugan Jain and P. S. Surana (trans. and eds.). 2011. *Jain Legend*, Jaipur: Samyagjñāna Pracāraka Mandala.

The Editors of Encyclopedia Britannica. 2019. "Chandragupta." *Encyclopedia Britannica*. Encyclopedia Britannica, Inc. https://www.britannica.com/biography/Chandragupta (accessed April 28, 2019).

Turner, Victor. 1968. "Religious Specialists." *International Encyclopedia of the Social Sciences* 13: 437–444.

United Nations, Department of Economic and Social Affairs, Population Division. 2013. *World Population Prospects: The 2012 Revision, Key Findings and Advance Tables*. Working Paper No. ESA/P/WP.227.

Vallely, Anne. 2002. "From Liberation to Ecology: Ethical Discourses among Orthodox and Diaspora Jains." *Jainism and Ecology: Nonviolence in the Web of Life*, Christopher Key Chapple (ed.). Cambridge: Harvard University Press.

Vijayendrasuri. 1960. *Tirthankar Mahāvīra*, Part 1. (1st edition). Bombay: Kashinath Sarak.

______. 1962. *Tirthankar Mahāvīra*, Part 2. Bombay: Kashinath Sarak.

Weber, Max. 1963. *The Sociology of Religion*. Boston: Beacon Press.

Wiley, Kristi L. 2004. *Historical Dictionary of Jainism*. Lanham, MD: Scarecrow Press.

Index

Ācārāṅga Sūtra, 18, 20, 113
Adipurāna (Jain text citing environmental ethics), 20, 34
Ahimsa (Non-violence; ecological applications), 14-15, 18, 21, 25, 114
Aindra Vyākaraṇa (Grammar text attributed to Mahāvīra), 37-38
Anekāntavāda (Doctrine of Pluralism), 18, 19, 80, 82
Aparigraha (Non-accumulation), 18, 21, 108
Ascetic practices (Mahāvīra's penance practices), 24, 41-44, 52, 59-61
Aśoka, Emperor, 21, 98, 99

Bahul (Brahmin donor of food), 43, 50
Bhagavati Sūtra, 35

Chandakauśika (Snake reformed by Mahāvīra), 47-49
Chandanā (Mahāvīra's first female disciple), 59, 63, 72, 95-96
Chetak (Ruler of Licchavikas; Mahāvīra's maternal uncle), 30
Climate change, 15, 18, 106, 114

Dharma, 14, 88, 104, 105, 109
Diet and veganism, 24, 25, 114
Digambara sect, 10, 31, 34, 35, 38, 43, 63, 97
Dīkṣā (Renunciation; Mahāvīra's initiation into asceticism), 41

Ecology, 103-105, 108
Ecumenical Spirit (Early Jain-Hindu-Buddhist syncretism), 29
Environmental Ethics, 101-103

Fasting (Mahāvīra's 12-year penance regimen), 41, 47, 49-61

Gaṇadharas (Mahāvīra's chief disciples), 63
Gandhi, Mahatma, 15, 18, 21

Gautama (Indrabhūti, Mahāvīra's primary disciple), 63, 69-78, 82-87, 92
Gender in Jainism, 32, 33
Gośāla, Makkhali (Rival ascetic), 50-56, 72-74
Greendex Survey, 16

Hastīmal, Acharya, 34, 38-40, 90, 100
Historical disputes in Jain literature, 26-27

Indian traditions and vegetarianism, 14, 16
Indra (King of gods), 34, 37, 43
Intellectual non-violence, 18

Jain cosmology, 17-20
Jain laypersons and professions, 20
Jain vegan movement, 24-25, 114
Jain virtue ethics, 14-22, 24-25
Jamāli (Disciple who later split), 64, 71, 74
Jinas vs. Tīrthaṅkaras, 26
Jñātragrām, 36

Kalpa Sūtra, 35
Karma theory, 54, 56, 65, 69-71, 77, 83, 85-86
Keval Jñāna (Omniscience), 62-88
Kṣatriya, 30-32, 45
Kundalpur/Kṣatriyakund (birthplace), 35-36

Licchavikas, 30
Liberation (Mokṣa), 10, 43, 102
Lokā and *Alokā* (Jain cosmology), 17, 29, 69
Lay Jains (Philanthropic and environmental roles), 18, 22, 102

Mahāvīra:
- Ascetic life, 42-44
- Adolescence, 37
- Biography and historiography, 26-28
- Conception and birth, 29-36
- Liberation (Parinirvāṇa), 91-97
- Marriage debate, 38-39
- Omniscience years, 62-88
- Parents, 36-37
- Public renunciation (Dīkṣā), 41-42

Mahāvīra Wildlife Sanctuary, 23, 113
Marriage and celibacy debate, 38-39
Martin Luther King Jr., 15
Monastic Practices: Ascetic disciplines, 41-61

Nandivardhan (Mahāvīra's brother), 41, 42
Non-theistic Religions: Jainism and Buddhism, 14
Non-violence (Ahimsa), 14-17

Omniscience, 30, 42, 43, 57, 58, 62-88, 96

Panch Kalyāṇaka (Five milestones of Tīrthaṅkaras), 10
Parinirvāṇa (Mahāvīra's Liberation), 91-97
Pārśvanātha: 23rd Tīrthaṅkara; predecessor, 57, 64
Penance: Mahāvīra's 12-year austerities, 41-61
Philosophy vs. religion (critique of Western categories), 13
Pollution and Indian rivers, 15
Pratikraman ritual, 22

Ramakrishna and gender transformation, 33
Renunciation, 41-42

Sallekhanā (fast till death), 41
Śankha: King who rescued Mahāvīra, 56
Sectarian Differences (Digambara vs. Śvētāmbara views), 9-10, 30-39, 43, 97
Siddhārtha (Mahāvīra's father), 36
Sustainability (Jain ethics), 13-25
Śvētāmbara sect, 26, 31, 32, 34, 38, 43, 97

Tīrthaṅkara
  Distinction from Jina, 26
  Mahāvīra as 24th, 29
  Others before him, 26, 27, 29
  Years as Tīrthaṅkara, 62-88
Triśalā (Mahāvīra's mother), 30, 36
Turner, Victor (liminality and charismatic leaders), 30

Veganism, 24, 25, 114
Vegetarianism, 14, 15, 18, 23, 106, 107, 108, 109
Videha kingdom (Region of Mahāvīra's birth), 35
Virtue ethics (Jain), 13-21

Weber, Max, (religious sociology) 13, 30
Women and Jain liberation, 33